ADVANCED PRAISE

"If you want to be inspired by one
ativity, and out-of-the-box thinking
his humble beginnings on the fam
cessful business ventures and the w.
a creative flare and visionary thinking to everything he does. He
sees opportunity in every challenge and exemplifies leadership by
putting his money where his mouth is. *Beyond Elon* documents a
remarkable journey of collaboration, risk taking and disruption of
status quo thinking. It shows us what is possible when you have
the passion, enthusiasm, drive, and commitment to making a difference in this world."

Dr. Andrew Weaver, award winning climate scientist
and author of *Generation Us: The Challenge of Global Warming*

"Loaded with practical advice and positively bubbling with
optimism as well as dashes of humor nestled amongst candid
anecdotes of colossal successes and lessons learned from the mis-
steps that led to the next open door, Jerry's personal story shares
his exceptional versatility across many industries to create an
inspirational and useful playbook for both emerging and established entrepreneurs."

Dave Olson, former Vice President of
Community and Marketing at Hootsuite, poet, podcaster,
postcard enthusiast, and pioneer of dozens of start-ups around
ecology, internet, and movie production

"*Beyond Elon* is a compelling story from Jerry Kroll, a pioneer of the electric vehicle industry who dares to think big things and make them happen. It is a story of resilience, determination, obsession, inspiration, genius, and, as the title suggests, a future beyond the status quo. With his latest company Jevitty, this remarkable man has turned his attention to improving and extending the human lifespan. As Jerry takes us on a journey through his life and career, he explains our potential for longevity and underlines the urgency of innovation in all sectors. It's a fun, fast ride that leaves you feeling like a brighter, more vibrant future is as inevitable and unstoppable as the electric car."

Wayne Moriarty, athlete, writer, journalist,
former Editor-in-Chief of *The Province*

"*Beyond Elon* is a provocative, hopeful business manifesto that shares a vision for humanity's future."

—*Foreword* Clarion Review

Pure Life!

BEYOND ELON:

The Next Great EV and Living Past 200

BY JERRY KROLL

with KELLY TATHAM

 FriesenPress

One Printers Way
Altona, MB R0G 0B0
Canada

www.friesenpress.com

ISBN
978-1-03-916861-9 (Hardcover)
978-1-03-916860-2 (Paperback)
978-1-03-916862-6 (eBook)

1. HEALTH & FITNESS, LONGEVITY

Distributed to the trade by The Ingram Book Company

TABLE OF CONTENTS

I dedicate this book to my amazing wife Naz.

They say that to live a long, healthy life you must have inspiration and passion.

For me, that is you.

*There's nothing more powerful
than an idea whose time has come.*

INTRODUCTION

I get it all the time whenever someone recognizes me as the founder and inventor of the Solo EV: "You're almost like Elon Musk!" It's a natural comparison to make, considering that Elon is the most famous electric car innovator in the world. Or at least it was a natural comparison to make … but since TikTok isn't available for me to buy and my response to the question, "Should Donald Trump's Twitter account be reinstated?" is a resounding "Hell no!" I now correct people when they tell me that I'm "almost Elon."

I'm not *almost* Elon. I'm the one and only Jerry Kroll. And I'm here to offer you something *beyond* Elon. Something new. Something different. Something better.

While I'm personally flattered by the comparison to Elon, I understand why not everyone would want to be associated with him. It's easy for me to have a soft spot—a blind spot even—for Elon Musk. I know what an incredible amount of dedication and energy it takes to bend the arc of history, to pull the future forward. Because whatever you think of Elon's antics and his personality, you can't deny his accomplishments.

Accomplishments like delivering us the cheapest solar panels in the world, building an electric car company that forced the car industry to shift to clean energy in a hurry, and launching satellite internet services across the globe that help people on the front lines of disaster stay safer by giving them the ability to communicate with the outside world.

Innovating at that level is not easy or straightforward. It requires more stamina and determination than most people know. You can't understand the pushback unless you've innovated at that level yourself.

We live in a culture that encourages the mocking, belittling, and otherwise disparaging of public figures. We put people on pedestals only to knock them down. You're a hero until you're a villain. How easy is it to type out critique after critique and how difficult is it to build something that makes a real impact on the world?

I'm not saying this to judge or condemn anyone's critiques. I'm saying this to shed light on the truth. Our society isn't set up to support dreamers and visionaries. It's set up to tear them down. That's why people give up on their dreams. That's why people feel it's too difficult to even start. That's why people believe dystopia is inevitable.

Some say that dystopia is part of Elon's plan, with his rocket ships and desire to build civilization on Mars, but I disagree. Giving up on Earth is not the point of becoming an interplanetary species. The point of becoming an interplanetary species is to keep Earth as home, not leave Earth behind. Besides, there isn't enough time to "leave Earth behind" anyway. We only have a decade or two to turn the climate situation around. If we don't undertake drastic changes in the next five, ten, twenty years … it's not, "Bye-bye Earth, we're going somewhere else," it's, "Bye-bye interplanetary potential and bye-bye human life."

As exciting as it must be to build rocket ships, the argument that right now most, if not all, of our efforts should be focused on fixing Earth and safeguarding our health is correct. A rocket ship is just an empty vessel until you put a human inside of it to experience awe and wonder.

What will really allow us the potential to become an interplanetary species is innovation around human health and longevity. Obviously, we don't get to go play on other planets until we've made Earth a safe and healthy place for home base—and!— until we've succeeded at safeguarding ourselves against aging. That's what gets us to Mars and beyond: extending our lifetimes—to two hundred years or longer.

Right now, with a ticking time limit of eighty to one hundred years, we're only living out a fraction of our potential. But, fortunately, thanks to dedicated scientists, doctors, researchers, innovators, and entrepreneurs around the world, you and I will be able to explore the infinite cosmos one day.

This is where I feel the biggest disconnect from Elon. He's publicly admitted to not understanding the benefits of human longevity. "I don't think we should try to have people live for a really long time," he told an interviewer in 2022, going on to rationalize that "most people don't change their mind[s]. They just die. So, if they don't die, we will be stuck with old ideas and society wouldn't advance" (Döpfner).

That's a bit of a weak argument from a man who holds the power to alter and advance society, don't you think? The truth is, we have most—if not all—of the solutions for climate change, poverty and hunger, homelessness, addiction, and systemic inequality. Meanwhile, we're close to achieving the solutions for all disease and death. The only thing we're lacking in solving the world's problems is support, resources, and willpower. All we must do is commit to working together, and we can get it all done.

I'm not giving up on Earth. I'm not giving up on humanity. And I'm also not giving up on the importance of risk-taking role models. Even when they demonstrate their bias and blind spots.

Daring innovators—like Elon and myself, Richard Branson, Warren Buffet, and so many more—stoke passions and imaginations of people of all ages around the world, showing them that "impossible" is just a word.

We empower people to act, to follow their dreams, take risks, and chase goals—but we also must admit that we're reaching for a world *beyond* the necessity of role models. We're reaching for a world where we don't need people like me to activate others. A world where innovation is the norm. A world where big dreams and lofty goals aren't just encouraged—they're the status quo. You want to build a paradigm-shifting business? Sounds good, Sally. Here's your starter kit packed full of everything you need to succeed. Now get out there and get it done!

That is the world I want to live in. That is the world I believe in and that is the world I know is possible.

In this book are the stories of how I came to believe in that world—the stories of how I learned to boldly follow my dreams, of trying to do great things for the planet and others. These are the stories of where those dreams led me, how I learned to connect the dots to see what is coming next, and why I'm throwing all my power behind that vision. I hope you enjoy reading, and I hope this book inspires you to believe in yourself and commit to *your* dreams and goals because you hold the power to pull a better future toward you—for yourself, and for all of us.

Full speed ahead!

THE MISSION

If you invest in the future, you'll be right.
If you invest in the past, you'll be wrong.

Sir John Templeton

As a child, I never understood why people had to die. I couldn't wrap my head around it. Death wasn't real to me. It didn't make sense. *I* was real. My parents, the flower farm I grew up on, my toy cars, the race car track down the highway ... all those things were real. But death? It bothered me. Where did we go, and why? It felt unnecessary, beside the point, and just plain stupid. I didn't fixate on it, but the question lived there, in the back of my mind, lurking: *Why does it have to be this way?*

If we had met when I was a young child, you might have tried to explain to me that death is part of the natural order of things. We are born, we live, and then we die. That's just the cycle of life. And if we had spoken back then about fossil fuels, you likely would have told me something else that many people accept as a natural part of life: that fossil fuels are necessary for humans to thrive.

We know for sure now that the latter statement is no longer true. We don't need to extract, refine, or burn fossil fuels in order to get from A to B, nor do we need fossil fuels in any other area of our lives. At least not for much longer—because while the transition from old to new energy is still under way, the tide has turned and there's no going back. It's only a matter of time before fossil fuels become obsolete. Just like death.

That's right. Death no longer has to be a part of the natural order of things. We can leave aging and dying behind, just like fossil fuels. I know it's hard to believe, but the writing is on the wall. It's only a matter of time before this information seeps into the public consciousness.

While it's obvious to me what's coming, I expect it might take you some time to accept the concept that humans will conquer aging. When I tell you that scientists have discovered why we age and how to slow down, halt, and even reverse the aging process (because aging is a *process*, not an inevitability), I know that some of you will push back. It's a normal and natural thing to do when you're confronted with a big, new idea.

I'm very familiar with pushback. I have been at the forefront of clean technology innovation building electric race cars, pioneering electric vehicle systems, and founding Electra Meccanica, the company behind the world's foremost single-seater electric car, the Solo, and the pushback I've received along the way has been astronomical.

Throughout my time developing electric vehicle systems, I've been laughed at, ignored, mocked, berated, and ridiculed. When I was creating the Solo, a car that is transforming the way we drive thanks to its compact size and utilitarian function, people did not understand it at all. When I approached the Canadian government for support in building what would have been Canada's first electric car manufacturing facility, their funding agents exchanged jokes behind my back, saying, "That's never going to happen." I had oil industry execs sit me down and tell me there's more energy in a cup full of gasoline than there'll ever be in an entire building full of electric batteries. People would tell me over and over again that there's no way battery cars would ever be successful. Even my own parents told me that they didn't believe electric cars would become a reality in their lifetime.

You can only imagine the look on their faces when I drove up to visit them in my first electric car—let alone showed them the first electric car I'd built myself!

It's been a challenging journey, learning to innovate against the pushback, but it got me to where I am today. Growing up in rubber boots and blue jeans, working every single day in a dark, cold greenhouse for a family who couldn't always pay their bills and with parents who sometimes had to feed my siblings and I jam sandwiches for breakfast, lunch, and dinner, I never imagined I'd end up here, talking to you about the parallels between the pushback against electric cars and the pushback against human longevity.

When I left home in my VW Scirocco with a few hundred bucks in my pocket to launch my first business from scratch, I had no idea that one day I would take multiple companies public, earn millions of dollars, and have the opportunity to retire young (but choose to keep working because retirement's kind of pointless if the planet's unlivable). I never dreamed that I would spend all my money (and then some) investing in projects I believed could change the world, that I would run for government with a Nobel Prize-winning scientist, or launch an app, an investment fund, and a business to expand human life potential exponentially. All I knew back then was that I wanted to make something of my own—something of value.

The path wasn't clear or straight and it certainly wasn't always easy. The only reason I've achieved the success I have today is because

I stayed positive and focused on my vision—and because I built a community of people around me who also believed in making the impossible possible.

Some of the feedback we've received while starting my latest company Jevitty Life Science—the app and investment fund for human longevity potential—has been just as bad as the feedback was with electric cars. Electric cars were laughed at, denied, underfunded, and recalled before finally being embraced and championed by the mainstream. Longevity is following the same trajectory. We're mostly still in the denial stage, but it won't be long before everyone starts to think about their lifespan differently.

At Jevitty, we're providing the playing ground for a new way of understanding how our lifestyle affects our lifespan. We're looking at—and measuring—how we eat, sleep, exercise, work, and play in order to expand our lives to make them longer, more fulfilling, balanced, and *fun*.

The Jevitty app measures your health and lifestyle metrics and provides a prediction of the length of your lifespan. Right now, my Jevitty app says I'm going to live to 122.643 years old. To get this number, the algorithm takes the stats I give it—my gender, location, annual income, education, healthcare plan, and whether or not I smoke or drink alcohol—on top of measuring my daily stats like the amount of sleep I get, the steps I take, my activity and exercise, and my body's current metrics for weight, body fat, VO_2 max, and resting heart rate. All this information gives the algorithm a full picture of my lifestyle and allows it to predict my lifespan. The Jevitty app makes it easy and fun for me to play around with lifestyle choices, understand how they affect my health, and implement the changes I need to thrive.

That's our goal at Jevitty, to make it easy for you to take control of your best health. It's about using all the tools and technology at our disposal to create an optimal life for ourselves and everyone around us, which also means reimagining our sick care industries into true health care systems. Because what we have today for health care is not good enough—not even close.

Real health care is preventative. It's about assessing where you're at presently, not waiting until you get sick. Proactive health care looks at genetic precursors and environmental factors and investigates and understands how diet and lifestyle affect your life. The future of medicine is stopping diseases before they even start, just like when your Tesla pings you and asks you to take it into the shop. No more breakdowns on the side of the road. You, along with the help of Jevitty and your doctor, will be able to monitor your health so effectively that there will be no surprises or shake-ups, just consistently good health and vitality.

Right now, most of us don't have access to proper health care. Even if you have full health benefits or you live in a country with socialized medicine, unless you've taken it upon yourself to invest in your longevity, you're tapped into a sick care system. It is the sad, unfortunate truth that our "health care" systems are reactive, providing care only *after* our health has deteriorated. Today, if you walk into your family doctor's office without any ailments, they're going to kick you out, saying, "Hey, get out of here. We've got sick people to look after." That is *if* you even have access to a family doctor, which many people, even in a place like Canada, don't (BC Health Care Matters).

Our current health care paradigm is failing us, and a lot of people don't even see it as they're so used to living this way. We've accepted it as "just the way things are," but we don't have to do that anymore.

I have personally spent a lot of time and energy feeling upset about our current systems, the governments that regulate them, and the industries that benefit from harming people and the planet. This frustration is what motivated me to start my businesses. It's easy to get lost in the anger and disbelief of it all, but, ultimately, I make a choice each day to not let it weigh me down. Because I understand that there is too much work to do to get lost in those feelings.

Just like I can't get lost in the frustration of our political systems, I can't get upset when I bring up human longevity and people want to shut down the conversation, unable to entertain the notion of living to two hundred years old or beyond. You wouldn't believe all the weird reasons people come up with for not wanting to live longer, healthier lives. They argue with me that they are committed to vacating the planet because of some arbitrary number on their birth certificates. By their own justifications, they're okay with dying because they believe that one hundred years old is the cap for human life.

These conversations remind me of how the Canadian government talks about oil and gas. We've known for *how many* decades that burning oil and gas is not compatible with a livable planet, and yet in 2021 our Prime Minister was still saying things like, "Canada is a major oil and gas company," on stage at the United Nations Climate Conference. As if that's something we're proud of as a country. As if that's a reality we cannot change. As if that's "just the way things are."

Paradigm shifts like recognizing aging as a disease, not an inevitability, or transitioning from known to unknown energy sources, can be a lot to wrap one's head around. If you grew up using oil and gas and not interacting with different energy sources, it's easy to get confused and push back on the unknown. If you didn't grow up suspicious of death, the revelation that researchers and doctors and scientists have discovered a way to halt and reverse aging *is* pretty freaking surreal.

Eventually, everyone will get it. Everything is changing around us, faster and faster each day, and people become aware at their own pace. A lot of the population is stuck in fear and patterns of doing things the old way, just because that's how they've always done them. And I know that when people are freaked out by climate change and wealth inequality, it makes it difficult for them to understand the excitement of human longevity.

The truth is that the upcoming and ongoing paradigm shift in health care is beyond our wildest dreams. The science and research unfolding across the planet right now is phenomenal. As the director of the Life Sciences Institute at the University of British Columbia, Pieter Cullis, writes in *The Personalized Medicine Revolution,* "we will leave behind the natural evolutionary forces that our ancestors endured and embark on a self-directed future" (2-3).

Or take it from David Sinclair, leading longevity researcher at Harvard Medical School, who said, "The first person to live to 150 years has already been born," and then later qualified that statement in 2022 with, "I said that about five years ago. In the last five years, something extraordinary has happened—making me think it's not just 150 years. [Now] all bets are off" (*Is Aging Reversible?* TED Talk).

He's right. In the next few decades, we will see a total transformation around health care, medicine, and our understanding of aging. As longevity medicines and technology become ready and accessible to everyone, not only will we be able to galvanize ourselves—to slow down and stop the aging process—but we will also be able to reverse aging entirely. We will turn back the clock on cancer, dementia, heart disease, wrinkles, grey hair, and everything else you can imagine.

That means that on our two hundredth birthday, we won't just be alive, but we will be strong, healthy, mobile, and full of enough energy to enrich each other and the world around us. That is what we understand at Jevitty, and that is what we're committed to supporting: the fast-tracking of this progress. We're here to make longevity the status quo.

I can't think of anything more exciting than turning two hundred years old and having absolutely no one ask me, "What's your secret?" I don't want to be in the news for my "achievement" or on any "world's oldest" lists. I want my two hundredth birthday to be a perfectly natural, normal, *expected* occurrence. By the time I celebrate two centuries of being alive, there's a chance we won't even be counting the years anymore—at least not like we do today, what with death dictating so many aspects of how we live.

While hitting two centuries won't be a unique or rare achievement, I will be raising a toast to the scientists, doctors, and researchers who worked tirelessly to extend human longevity through decades of hard work in discovering the tools, techniques, and technology that allowed us to slow, halt, and reverse the aging process.

The last one hundred years have brought more change to the planet than humanity has ever seen before, and the change in the next one hundred years is going to blow the last century out of the water.

My goal is to live beyond two hundred years old and have nobody ask me how I did it. Now, let's dig into the stories of how I arrived at this goal so l can show you how it's not only possible, but simple for both me and you to ring in over two centuries on this planet.

Unless, of course, you'd rather celebrate the big two-oh-oh on Mars.

GROWING UP GREEN

*Discouragement and failure are two of
the surest stepping stones to success.*

Dale Carnegie

So, how does a guy like me take multimillion-dollar businesses public, get together with a Nobel Prize winner in environmental sciences to run for politics, and then launch a company that will help change the human race forever? How does a guy who didn't even graduate high school, let alone get a college education, accomplish all of these momentous feats? It all started in a greenhouse.

My story, just like my background, is unique. It's unlike anything anybody has ever done before—which is exactly the same for you and your background, along with everyone else in the world. That's the beauty of it. My story has shaped who I am and what I have to offer, just like your story shapes you. We all have something uniquely our own to offer. You could try to look into my background for a blueprint on how to be successful in business, but you wouldn't find it. When it comes to being successful in business, it's not about "how full is the bucket," but *what's in* the bucket that counts. It's about what makes you, you, and what perspective you bring to the table that no one else has.

My parents raised me to work hard, take risks, and not screw up. They were immigrants who took a big risk in coming to Canada to build a better life for their family. They imbued me with a relentless work ethic and can-do attitude, and they tolerated my enthusiasm for race cars. I owe them a lot.

They grew up in Hücklehoven, a small coal mining town in western Germany. In high school, my dad, Robert, studied to become a gardener. He loved plants and flowers and learning about their history and how to care for them, but by the time he got married to my mom, Balbina, he hadn't yet established himself in his preferred field. So instead, he went to work in the town's coal mine, where he could make money quickly. Shortly after starting work in the mines, he fell and got injured. This upset my mom, and right away she told him he couldn't go back and that they were either going to do the flower thing or nothing at all. He listened and they started a little flower shop in a small town about an hour away called Wuppertal. They had relative success and enjoyed the life they were creating together, but because of the housing market in Germany in the late fifties, they couldn't come close to affording the cost of a home.

In the 1950s, house prices in Germany were crazy, similar to what's going on in Canada (and many other places in the world) today. By the time my parents had two kids—my older brother and sister—they decided to emigrate somewhere where it would be easier for them to raise a family. They looked at Australia and Canada as options and ended up choosing Canada because friends from Holland had raved about the west coast of British Columbia. Their friends told them that once they touched down in Montreal, they should start driving and not stop until they got to Vancouver.

They loaded up their Volkswagen van with my older siblings, $500 in their pockets, and crossed the Atlantic, heeding their friends' advice and driving the then-gravel highway all the way across Canada until they hit the Pacific Ocean.

My family settled in Coquitlam, a town about an hour outside of Vancouver, and about six months after they arrived, I was born. My birthday is Christmas Day, 1960, which happens to be the same day that my older brother was born (a surprising commonality we share with Canadian Prime Minister Justin Trudeau and his brother: two Christmas babies in the same family). If you're wondering why my mother chose to undertake such an arduous journey while pregnant, let me tell you that it took me until adulthood to realize that my nickname "Booboo" wasn't in reference to the Yogi Bear cartoon.

As new Canadians, my parents decided not to speak German while they settled in. They figured speaking English was the best way to assimilate. Their neighbours were very friendly and supportive, bringing over pots and pans and other goods to help us get set up. Right away my dad got a job working in a local greenhouse while my mom worked to raise the kids. Over the next several years they saved up enough to buy their own parcel of land so they could start their own greenhouse business. In 1966, they bought two-and-a-half acres in Port Coquitlam for $2,000. Together as a family, we built the greenhouses and set up the flower farm. They launched their business the following year, but it took a couple of years to get it properly off the ground. In the meantime, my dad continued to work at his original job and my mom picked up night shifts as a cleaner at Simon Fraser University. There was no complaining about the long hours or double shifts. They kept their heads down and worked diligently toward their goals.

In the greenhouses, we grew flowers. Chrysanthemums became our bread and butter throughout the year, with vibrant red poinsettias added in during the fall to sell over the Christmas season.

We had rows upon rows of flowers, carefully bred and raised to go to auction, where brokers would bid on them. Business was unreliable but steady. It was a guessing game how much we'd earn—the nature of flower auctions being that you don't know how much you're going to make until the auction is underway. It could be $7 for one flowerpot or it could be $1. It would depend entirely on the demand, the quality of the competitors' flowers, and who showed up that day to buy. It wasn't the most lucrative business, but it made my parents happy. We had enough to get by, but money in our house was tight and jam sandwiches were often served for dinner.

Our greenhouse business was a true family-run business, and the five of us kids worked seven days a week. Every day before school we were up and out of bed in the dark mixing soil, potting flower cuttings, watering and tending to the growing plants. We'd put in at least an hour of work before school, and after school we'd work until it got dark with only a break to eat a jam sandwich. Then weekends we'd work all day. Once the business was established, my parents hired workers, but it turns out you can't get quite the same value from people who demand things like breaks and five-day work weeks. So, we would have people come in and out over the years, but us kids were the real backbone of the operation.

The only day of the year we didn't have to work was Christmas— my birthday, a magical day. Christmas Eve was great too because we only had to work half the day, and it was fun because there were lots of people around buying up the last of the poinsettias. It was the only time of the year I could go into the greenhouse without leaving cold and muddy. I loved soaking in that world and its beauty, lit up by the twinkly lights strung up for the holidays, appreciating all the hard work we had put in the rest of the year. I never resented my parents for working us so hard, and I recall most of my friends working for their parents as well. It was normal, and it most certainly gave me my work ethic.

Growing flowers was an art and a science. The growing process always started with getting just the right mixture for the soil: a blend of peat moss, perlite, sand, and sometimes a little lime. You'd have to nail the blend to ensure you had good water retention and drainage. We'd do the mixing in a big container, a large drum that we would pour all the ingredients into. Once all the elements had been dumped inside, we'd close the lid and turn it on. It would spin around for about half an hour, and then we'd place a wheelbarrow underneath and press the button to release its contents.

We'd have tables upon tables throughout about an acre of greenhouses lined with pots, and we'd fill the pots with the soil mixture and plant cuttings. For the chrysanthemums, we'd have these little cuttings that needed to be planted in almost straight perlite for the roots to take hold. This would take about two weeks, and during that time we would top them off with more perlite, tamp them down, and keep them moist. It was quite an intensive process. I'd be out there with a garden hose day after day, sprinkling water on the cuttings to keep them cool, my dad always looking over my shoulder and telling me he'd unalive me if I didn't do it right. He never had to tell me twice. He scared me, and whether it was because of this or in spite of it, I had a sense of pride in getting it right. I wanted to make him proud, and I didn't mind the hard, meticulous work. I appreciated the challenge.

Though my parents never involved me in the business side of their work, I felt naturally drawn to salesmanship. The risk and the reward of not knowing exactly how much you would earn appealed to me. Buyers would come over, and my dad would negotiate back and forth with them until they landed on a price. Watching these business transactions enthralled me; I decided that I wanted to sell things too.

When I was about five or six years old, I launched my first business. Alongside our house, I found some rocks that I thought were extraordinarily pretty, so I polished them up until they were shiny and ready to sell. With these precious stones tucked into my pocket, I marched down the road to my neighbours' house to offer them a deal. I presented them with a handful of—I must say, truly spectacular—pebbles and requested a few dollars in exchange. The neighbours acquiesced and (perhaps I'm colouring the memory, but I'm pretty sure) they were genuinely delighted by their new purchases. I was incredibly proud of myself. It was my first business deal! I made something from nothing. But when I got home, pocket clanging with two or three dollars, my mom wanted to know where I had gotten the money from. When I explained to her, beaming with pride, what I'd done, she lost it. She was appalled that I had "hoodwinked" (her word) the neighbours. She saw my budding salesmanship as begging for money, and she made me go back and return my earnings immediately. I cried the whole way there. I didn't understand what I'd done wrong—clearly, I hadn't gotten the right permits in place.

While my mom was embarrassed, I got my first taste of the rush of sales. And I liked it.

While my personal sales career was stalled out for the time being, I still got to scratch the sales itch by helping my dad at the flower auctions. The auctions took place in a big warehouse called United Flower Growers. They were modelled after the flower auctions in Holland. A large Dutch community had built up the industry here. Before the auctions were put in place, farmers would bring their flowers straight to the brokers, and the brokers would rip them off left, right, and centre. They would undercut the farmers, offering them $0.20 for a pot that was worth at least $1.50. The farmers would have no choice but to sell their product at the set rates because the flowers were going to die otherwise. So, they'd end up selling them for way less than their value. On top of that, when it came time for the brokers to pay up, they would claim that half the flowers had died in order to get away with paying the farmers even less than they'd originally promised—basically peanuts to the dollar for what they were worth. So, being the game changers they are, the farmers revolted and built their own auction system.

Technically it wasn't an auction, but a reverse auction. There'd be a huge clock on the wall and a gallery full of buyers. Someone would wheel in a cart of flowers, and the auctioneer would say, "This flower is worth around $1, so we'll start the clock at $2." The clock would start ticking down from $2 to $1.99 to $1.98, and so on. It would go super fast. The buyers would have to guess and assess the demand in order to decide when to pounce, because whoever pressed the button first, stopping the clock, got as many flowers as they wanted. If you pressed it too soon, you ended up paying more than they were worth. Say you bought a bunch at $1.50 and then the clock got wound back up and nobody pressed the button again until it hit $0.50. You would have just wasted a bunch of money and you'd have a hard time reselling the flowers at a decent margin. It's very much like a casino, and learning that psychology from an early age served me well in business.

I'd often be late for school after the auctions, but my teachers didn't mind because they knew I was working. I attended Glen Elementary School and Mary Hill Junior Secondary School—schools semi-famous for educating Terry Fox. Terry was two years older than me, and we played football on the same team. Terry was an intimidating figure back then. I remember me and some other kids running away from him after he threatened to beat the crap out of us. He never actually did beat us up, but he liked to scare the hell out of us younger kids. I don't think you can accomplish what he did without a bit of a chip on your shoulder. (On a longevity note, oncologists have stated that if Terry's battle with cancer had taken place today, he wouldn't have died, let alone even lost his leg. That's how far medicine has advanced in the past forty years.)

Unimpressed by the school system, I ended up dropping out of high school just before the eleventh grade. It just didn't interest me. At my school in 1975, most of the teachers simply did not care. They didn't care if you were listening. They didn't care if you did the homework. They didn't even care if you were there. I remember some of the teachers starting class, handing out work for us to do, and then leaving to go golfing. Seriously! They'd leave us there alone and unsupervised to fill out pointless worksheets as they putted around the neighbourhood green. And you could feel that they hated being there as much as I did and that they had no interest in me or any of my classmates. Of course, there were one or two exceptions, teachers who were really fine people. But otherwise, you could tell that they hated their jobs, and they definitely took that frustration out on us.

I do remember one teacher who was genuinely decent, a met-alwork teacher in high school, Mr. Reeves. He was one of those fantastic teachers you keep in the back of your mind that give you hope for our education system. I had my mind set on making a steel "wagon wheelbarrow" for my greenhouse—something useful, something I would actually use. I had the idea to create a con-traption that had wheelbarrow handles in the front and layers of shelves where I could stack boxes of flowers. I designed it all by myself. I was about fourteen at the time, figuring out how to do this on my own. I chopped up all the steel and started putting it together. Mr. Reeves would take the class to different areas of the of the shop, showing them how to do this and that. I would fade into the background and start working on my things by myself. I kept waiting for him to yell at me, "Hey, get over here." But he never did. He just let me work quietly away on my project. I thought for sure I was going to get an F because I didn't do the assignment, but he ended up giving me an A because he was a big fan of my enthusiasm. He even told me that when he gave me my grade! That was encouraging, but that experience was the exception to the rule.

I can still recall the exact moment I knew school was no longer for me. I was standing in our family driveway the summer before tenth grade when suddenly the air went out of the whole thing, just deflated. I had been so excited to go back to school, and then out of nowhere it was like a light switched off. I realized instead that all I wanted was to be in business. The idea of school left me completely cold. Nothing was happening in that place. It felt like I was just going there to put in time. Like prison.

Fortunately, my mom and dad got it. There was no pushback from them on that front. They understood it wasn't worth my time, and they were thrilled to have me as a full-time employee. I was happy to work for them—I wanted to work—and I was ready to take on more responsibility and learn the ropes of running a business.

Looking back, I can see now that this was the first time I took a big risk based on a gut feeling. Finishing high school is kind of the bare minimum for most people, but I knew it wasn't for me. I knew I didn't need a diploma to be successful in my life. However, I recognize that I'm an outlier. Even the Jevitty app tells me that I'd live longer if I had a college degree. Heck, the algorithm says that having a master's or doctorate will add seventeen years to my lifespan (because they would boost the likelihood that I earn more and therefore have better access to healthy lifestyle choices and proper health care). But dropping out of high school got me to where I am today, building a company that will extend my lifespan exponentially. Math can't always account for variances like that.

In the end, we have to trust our guts *and* keep working on the algorithm to make it more nuanced and attuned to what makes individual humans thrive.

Growing up wasn't all flowers and failed rock sales. The best part about living on the acreage in Port Coquitlam was that it was a mile away from the racetrack—a famous racetrack called Westwood. Westwood Motorsport Park was designed by Sir Sterling Moss, one of the greatest race car drivers of the '40s, '50s, and '60s, and oh boy, was it ever epic. At least it felt that way to me the first time my dad took me there. I was seven years old, and it was the most exciting thing in the world.

Those days, the track was surrounded by forest, nestled on the corner of Westwood Street and Lougheed Highway. On the way home from the grocery store, we would pass a wooden sign that said *Coming Soon! Cars, Motorcycles, and Go Karts*, with the dates listed below. So I knew exactly when the cars were coming and I lobbied my dad hard to take me. I didn't ask politely either. I demanded to see the cars.

It was his fault anyway. After my folks took us to see *The Love Bug* at the local cinema, I was beside myself with excitement to see the real thing. It consumed my mind. I begged and begged and begged my dad until he finally agreed.

We'd go to the racetrack around lunchtime—the main races were usually from one o'clock to three o'clock—and once we got back home, we'd have to work late to make up for the missed time. Unlike the occasional BC Lions game he'd take me to where the game started after work was done for the day, going to the race-track ate into daylight hours, so him granting me this privilege was a special occurrence. Working late afterwards was always worth it.

I'd fly through my tasks, all revved up on adrenaline, replaying the races over and over again in my head.

Up in the mountains in Coquitlam, the races didn't actually have that many people in attendance. Not like car races today. The track was pretty primitive back then, with no protective barriers or anything between the track and the audience. You had to stay clear or you'd get hit, which only added to the excitement. It was loud and noisy and made me feel completely alive. I was enthralled by the whole thing.

We'd watch from the stands, where the Export A girls in their little outfits would circulate, handing out cigarette samples. They would walk up and down the aisles of the grandstand, handing out packages of cigarettes to everyone—including me, a seven-year-old. And nobody batted an eye. That's how different things were back then. Back then they still ran cigarette commercials in between *The Flintstones* cartoons, basically encouraging kids to start smoking. I took my little pack of three cigarettes home and lit one. It was a stupid idea, so thankfully it didn't take. My mom and dad didn't smoke. We knew people who smoked, but I figured it was kind of a dumb thing to do. Fortunately, the laws have changed so that they don't allow those kinds of promotions anymore. I don't think I need to tell you that smoking cigarettes is a huge deterrent to good health and longevity. We all know this by now.

Besides the cigarettes, they'd also give out a single-page program that listed all the cars and who was driving them. The first time we went, my dad pointed out the Porsche on the list. That was the first time I'd heard that word: Porsche. He said it was going to be amazing, but when it came out, I was disappointed. My dad explained that it actually wasn't a real Porsche after all and that maybe we'd see one next year. The next time we went back, we did get to see the real thing. That Porsche was a monster. It was a beautiful white car with red and blue stripes, and it completely destroyed everything else on the track.

One car did steal my imagination that first year—a Corvette driven by Jerry Olson. It was fast and sexy, a muscly car, and it was driven by someone with my name! That sealed the deal for me. I became officially obsessed and started dreaming about race cars: watching them, driving them, and maybe one day even building them.

Around the same time that I discovered race cars, I began to develop an interest in sustainable energy technology. I was particularly taken by the Grumman company and their solar panels. I must have read about them in *Popular Mechanics* or some other kids' magazine. I was so struck by the concept of solar energy that I wrote Grumman a letter without my parents knowing, asking them about their technology. When I received an amazing and inspiring information package back from some good soul at Grumman in the mail, my parents asked me, "What are you doing? Where is this coming from?"

I liked the idea of working with nature, using resources that weren't extracted. Maybe it was growing up in the greenhouse, creating something from nothing, watching those tiny little plant cuttings grow into beautiful flowers that in turn would support our whole family. I was learning the value of sunlight and time, and that sparked an interest in me. I remember seeing how much gas the greenhouse needed to keep running. I had no idea back then that gasoline was so bad for the planet; I just knew it was expensive. I figured if you had to spend $100 on gas every month, but you could spend $1,000 on solar panels that would replace the gas for all the foreseeable months, then why wouldn't you invest in solar panels? After ten months, you're making money. It's a no-brainer. Why would you keep pouring funds into something when you didn't have to?

Not long after I wrote to Grumman about solar panels, my dad gave me a set of Hot Wheels for my birthday. It was the 1970s, and they were Hot Wheels Sizzlers, an electric version where the cars came with built-in motors and tiny rechargeable batteries. You would plug the cars into their charging station, and then they would drive all by themselves on a Hot Wheels track. Naturally, it was the coolest thing ever. As I played with them, I started wondering why we didn't have full-scale cars like this in the real world. Why fill a car with stinky, expensive gas when you could plug it into the wall for next to nothing? I swear to you, that's where I got the idea for my electric car company. I knew from a very young age what made sense, and those ideas and understandings never left me.

After dropping out of high school, I worked at the family greenhouse for nearly eight years, from fifteen to twenty-two years old. When I left school, I thought it was going to be a great thing for me to work full-time for my parents. As it turned out, it wasn't nearly as much fun as I had expected. In the beginning, I was so enthusiastic, doing everything they told me to do—and it was hard work nonstop—but that enthusiasm began to fade over time. I never got to dress in clean clothes like I would for school, and I was always covered in dirt, always exhausted and cold. But the part that *really* bothered me was that I didn't get to participate in any of the business aspects of running the greenhouse. I was truly their employee, there to haul dirt and pot plants, not to participate in any sort of entrepreneurial way. I was ready to cut deals. I wanted to wager and negotiate. I wanted to run logistics. I kept angling to get more involved in the business side of things, but no matter what I did, my parents kept deflecting.

When I pitched them horticulture college, I told them I would go and learn everything I needed to know to run a greenhouse business, but they said no. Then I heard a story about a neighbour who'd also worked for his family's greenhouse business. The family had around twelve greenhouses, and his father offered his son one greenhouse to take control of and run on his own, sort of an operation within the operation to test drive his abilities. I loved that idea. I thought I could convince my parents to let me take on the tiniest portion of their business. I ran it by my dad, pitching it to him wide-eyed and excited. He shut me down immediately. He didn't even care to hear the full pitch. "Absolutely not," he said. "We just don't do that."

That's when I realized I needed to leave—or at least that's when I began to wake up to the fact that there was no future for me in my parents' greenhouse business. It wasn't an official epiphany moment like when I quit high school. It was more of a slow transition into drudgery and the understanding that it was very much my parents' business and was always going to be my parents' business. As a young man, I had been under the misguided perception that they were just going to hand the business down to me at some point. That's the tradition for many families, and I thought it would be the same for us. But the greenhouses were their retirement plan. And I had no intention of buying the business from them after working to build it.

Looking back, I have the utmost gratitude for my parents being so firm about not letting me get involved. The greenhouse business clearly wasn't for me. It was all I knew, and I couldn't see beyond it, so they did me a great service in saying no to my requests. For the first ten years after I left, I had nightmares about being back in rubber boots, cold, and covered in dirt, working away into the dark of night. That was not the life for me.

It took a year or two after my dawning realization before I actually got out. Around the time my eyes opened, I had just spent all my savings on a Volkswagen Scirocco, and it took a while to save up again. But once I did, it was pure freedom. It was 1983 and I had my Scirocco, a few hundred bucks in my pocket, and boundless energy and passion. While I wasn't ready to *fully* fly the coop just yet, I was ready to make something of my own.

I moved out, but I stayed in the flower business because it was the only business I knew. I moved out of the greenhouse and into sales, launching my own flower brokerage business from scratch. I ate, breathed, and slept flowers. I would work from five in the morning until eight o'clock at night, seven days a week. The first time my parents came over to my new apartment my mom opened the fridge to find it filled, top to bottom, with daffodils. She laughed and laughed. It was exciting for her to see me, if you'll pardon the pun, *blooming* like this.

I got my product from the United Flower Growers auction in South Burnaby—the same one I'd been going to since I was a little boy. Everybody there knew me, and I knew just when to call "stop" on the auction clock. I hustled to get the best flowers to broker around town.

I loved being in charge of setting my own prices, and because I had no overhead (all the other brokers had big warehouses and trucks and employees while I just had my fridge and my VW), I could buy a pot for $0.50 and sell it for $1. Meanwhile, the other wholesalers were selling the same pot for $3. I didn't need the big markup like they did, and I didn't care that I was undercutting them.

All of a sudden, every florist was calling me up, asking me to bring them flowers, begging to get their hands on my product. People were buying my stock like crazy—which of course meant that the other wholesalers got pretty upset with me. They told me I should always ask what price the other brokers are selling at to keep the market steady, but I knew exactly what I was doing. How do you think Richard Branson got Virgin Records off the ground? Sometimes, you have to be a disrupter to launch yourself and your business.

Business grew so fast it was bonkers. It wasn't long before I was buying trucks and hiring employees. I would spend my weekends installing shelving in the trucks and planning out the best routes, while my weeks were full of hiring employees, training them, and sending them out to work. I started opening my own flower shops and delivering to local grocery stories—Woodward's and Safeway—and even began exporting to Seattle. My services were in high demand. It was exhilarating.

You might expect a twenty-two-year-old guy to be out partying or clubbing or chasing women, but I did none of that. I wasn't distracted by social things or girlfriends or anything of the sort. All I cared about was building my business. I worked around the clock, but it never felt like work—to me, it was fun. Growing up, my heroes were Howard Hughes and Jimmy Pattison (a local big business entrepreneur), not Dean Martin or Frank Sinatra. It was the innovators, the entrepreneurs, and the business guys who inspired me. Building my own company was all I cared about, and returning home to my very own bachelor apartment, paid for with the money I made from my own business, was the only high I needed.

I did this for years before it dawned on me that while I was doing a lot of really good work, I was not making a lot of net profit. When I started to notice people doing a lot better financially than me while working a lot less, the wheels in my head started to turn. Growing up on the farm, all I knew was hard labour. It hadn't occurred to me that there wasn't necessarily a correlation between how hard you work and how much money you make. On top of that, I was getting bored of flowers. They didn't capture my attention the way they used to, and because of that, the work was getting harder.

Around that time, I attended a Brian Tracy conference. Tracy is a motivational speaker, and at the time they were franchising his talks, so you'd just show up to this big room and watch a recording of him on a screen. On the drive back from the talk, it hit me—I would always be grateful to my parents and the flower business for teaching me so much, but flowers weren't my true passion. When I got really honest with myself, I realized I didn't give a crap about the flower business. I thought about what I really loved—what I would *pay* to do—and I realized it was car racing.

I knew it would take time to get there, that I would have to build up my skillset and establish myself first, but I had a pretty good idea of how to do it. Brian Tracy talked about this a lot—if you're doing the right thing, people will be pulled toward you. From that moment forward, as I set my sights on doing what I truly loved, I committed to taking the right steps along the way: staying positive, working hard, and being friendly and welcoming to everyone around me.

We all deserve to follow what we're truly passionate about. We all deserve to do what we love. I knew that for me it was time to go forward. It was time to work in motorsports!

THE FAST LANE

There are three sports in the world:
bullfighting, mountain climbing, and
car racing.
Everything else is a game.

Ernest Hemingway

While I was working as a flower broker, I joined the Burnaby Chamber of Commerce in order to garner a higher profile for the florist franchise and make connections with other business people in the area. Unlike some people, I actually enjoy networking—*especially* when food is involved. Lucky for me, the Burnaby Chamber of Commerce had regular breakfast networking meetings.

This was the late 1980s, when IndyCar had been courting the City of Vancouver for a while in attempts to set up an annual race event. Vancouver, however, was refusing to commit. The city was waffling back and forth, dragging their feet on the opportunity. One morning, I was sitting in my office reading the paper in advance of a Chamber meeting and I flipped the page open to yet another article about how the City of Vancouver didn't think IndyCar would "work" for the community because of whatever silly excuse they were coming up with that day, and a lightbulb went off in my head.

I arrived at the meeting and sat down—plate full of snacks—with a subcommittee made up of the heads of all the shopping malls in Burnaby. It was me, one other gentleman, and several female mall managers and business owners, brainstorming ideas on how to drive traffic to the shopping malls and discussing the possibility of a tech fair, when it popped out of my mouth: "What do we think about Burnaby hosting an annual IndyCar race?"

Everyone in the group's eyes widened. As I tried to decipher their expressions, more words spilled out of my mouth. I told them that IndyCar had been lobbying the city for a while and that they were super interested in coming to town, but Vancouver kept throwing up roadblocks. I told them that Burnaby stood a real shot of hosting IndyCar instead. As I finished my spiel, I watched as their widened eyes turned into huge smiles.

While I didn't know what to expect, I certainly didn't think I would receive such an outrageously positive reaction. I was worried that pitching IndyCar was kind of like suggesting we go to Mars. I thought they might wrinkle their noses and say, "Boo. Get out of here with your vroom vroom stuff." So, when their widened eyes turned into wide smiles and everyone around the table told me that they absolutely *loved* the idea, I was beside myself with excitement.

After the committee told me that they were 100% behind me and encouraged me to "go for it," they gave me a signed letter backing the idea. I took the letter to Elwood Veitch, who was the MLA for the Burnaby-Willingdon riding at the time, and as luck would have it, he loved the idea too. Not only did he love it, but he said he could allocate a million dollars to bringing an IndyCar race to Burnaby. I took my letter and Elwood's promise and went to meet with Bill Copeland, the mayor of Burnaby. Bill was equally as thrilled. He said he'd arrange an additional million dollars to make it happen. I was floored. I could hardly believe it.

As Elwood and Bill started pulling the finances together, I met with a PR guy named Roy Adams from Molson Canada (the beer company) at the big factory brewery on Burrard Street in Vancouver and told him that the Burnaby Chamber of Commerce, the province of British Columbia, and the City of Burnaby were all on board. Naturally, Molson was just as thrilled as we all were, so the PR guy phoned up IndyCar and told them that we were serious about bringing the series in—and that we had all our ducks in a row.

Next thing I knew, John Frasco, the CEO of CART (Championship Auto Racing Teams), was flying in from Detroit to take a look around. We welcomed him in and toured the area together, showing him where we had the track planned out and meeting with all the folks who were lining the money up. It was smooth and fast and easy. Everything was good to go. We all shook hands, and the City of Burnaby looked all set to bring the IndyCar race to town.

What happened next and what those who lived in Vancouver in the '90s will remember is that the City of Vancouver had a seven-day shotgun clause. Even though they'd been dragging their feet—or, pardon me, "doing prep work"—Vancouver still had the first right of refusal. After shaking hands with Burnaby, John Frasco went into the city and told them their seven days started now.

With this fire lit under their butts, Vancouver activated their right to host the series, and the Molson Indy Vancouver event was launched. The circuit ran every summer from 1990 to 2004 near downtown Vancouver in False Creek. While I was disappointed that Burnaby didn't get it, what really mattered was that IndyCar was coming to town for everyone to enjoy—and I'd witnessed just how quickly and smoothly you can achieve momentum behind an idea that you're truly passionate about.

During the time Molson Indy Vancouver found its feet and got off the ground, I was still in the flower game. I had about seventeen flower shops across the Lower Mainland (once I'd been successful with my own flower brokering, I figured it was time to expand my brand), but the flower franchise business wasn't working out as I'd hoped. It wasn't just boredom showing me the door; it was also frustration over my struggle to properly franchise the business.

I called my flower franchise Celebrity Florist and modelled it after a flower franchise in California called Conroy's, who, at the time, had hundreds of locations. I spent some time in Los Angeles checking out what they were doing as they'd had a lot of success in placing their business on street corners, and figured I could probably pull off the same model in the Vancouver area.

I found my franchise owners by placing advertisements in the paper. Once they'd signed on, I'd help them set up the stores. I would show them the ropes, train them, answer questions, and offer ongoing support, but would otherwise leave it up to them to run the business. Meanwhile, they'd pay me royalties. Or at least that was the plan.

Flowers are not a great product to fit into a franchising model, especially when you don't have the flair for or understanding of the product. Despite the training and encouragement I gave, none of the franchisees seemed able to figure out what they were doing. I would drop by the stores to check in on them, and the counters would be empty, which I could never understand. If you went into a flower shop and it was empty, you would never go back, would you? So, nobody was paying me royalties because nobody was making any money. Running a flower business was second nature to me, but it turned out it wasn't a transferable skill.

Flowers aren't very sustainable as a franchise. How many flower franchises do you know of, compared to something like coffee shops? Coffee is something that a regular person buys every day—sometimes multiple times a day. But people don't buy flowers every day. That's a poetic thought, but not a real one. I buy a lot of flowers because I appreciate them, but it's more like two or three times a month. Successful franchises need to be something more repeatable—burritos or bread or something like that. With anything else, it's really tough to be successful.

I disbanded the franchises and walked away. I told the franchisees to do their own thing. Nobody was upset about it, and I never looked back. Part of being a good business person means knowing when to move on.

It didn't make sense to stay, but leaving was its own kind of risk. Suddenly, I was out in the world without a net. I had nothing lined up and no savings in the bank. IndyCar was coming to Vancouver, but I didn't know yet the role I would play in it. After I cut the franchise cords, I started to feel a bit nervous about how I was going to feed myself for the next little while.

As serendipity would have it, a new opportunity rushed in as soon as I let the old one go. I was walking down Howe Street the very same week that I walked away from the flower franchise, wondering to myself what I was going to do next, when I bumped into an old friend of mine. He asked me what I was up to, so I told him the truth—that I didn't know what was next yet. To that, he smiled and said, "I have these clients who just acquired this business doing a frozen yogourt franchise through the Canadian Franchise Association. Is that something you would be interested in running?"

I smiled at the synchronicity and said, "Heck yes, I'll take a meeting." Not only was the timing perfect, but the product was simple and straightforward. Frozen yogourt as opposed to delicate, perishable flowers? Come on. All you have to do is store it in a freezer. I knew immediately that this business would be much easier to run.

My friend put in a call to the owners, and I met with them right away. The owners were a couple of really charming older fellows, and when we met, I liked what I heard. I gave them an idea of what I'd do with their business, where I'd take it, how I'd run it, and all that good stuff. They said they'd get back to me in the next week.

I walked out of the meeting feeling pretty good about the chemistry and my chances of landing the job, and by the time I got to my car, my phone was ringing. It was them saying, "Can you start Monday?"

My immediate thought was, *Wow. It really pays to take risks*. I could have taken my time disbanding the franchises and trying to extract the money I was owed, but no. I knew it was time to move on. It can be scary to take those leaps, but you have to trust that your commitment to change will have your back. That opportunity never would have come up had I not turned away from something I knew wasn't right for me anymore. My Spidey senses can always tell if something is meant to be or not. Experiences like that have taught me to trust in the timing and to always stay focused on moving forward, without fear of how you're going to get there.

The frozen yogourt franchise was the easiest business I've run by a longshot. The owners loved me and appreciated my experience and business acumen, especially in dealing with people who had a hard time taking instructions. The owners were a delight to work for, and it was such a straightforward and enjoyable job. It was tough to walk away once my race car management and sponsor-ship work got off the ground.

My career in the race car world began as Molson Indy Vancouver was gearing up to its launch in 1990, but that work didn't hit full-time until 1992-93. The people who championed me into the IndyCar fold were a group of local businessmen and motorsports enthusiasts called the Spirit of Vancouver. As soon as the ink on the Vancouver Indy contract dried, they reached out and asked if I wanted to help them put a driver into the race.

This, of course, was exactly what I wanted to do.

I stayed working for the frozen yogourt guys as long as I could—probably longer than I should have—as the world of car racing began to take all of my energy and attention. Every time I tried to quit the yogourt franchise, they'd reduce my hours or offer me more money. That's how much they appreciated me and what I offered the company. By the time I officially left, I'd been travel-ling all over the world for racing and giving the bare minimum to the franchise. It finally got to the point where I was working like three hours a week for full-time pay, and I said to them, "I love you guys, but this isn't fair anymore. I have to leave the company. Good luck."

My new job was to raise money and land sponsorships for race car drivers. For the first Vancouver Indy, we needed $110,000 to pass "GO" and get our driver on the track. This was no easy feat. Luckily, building enthusiasm and getting people to give funds and sponsorships came naturally to me. And so began my career in car racing and my time spent working with the Spirit of Vancouver.

To get the ball rolling on fundraising, we'd host parties at the Granville Island Hotel and sell memberships to the Spirit of Vancouver for $25 a piece. For those who were keen to spend $100, they'd get a membership and a ticket to the race, where they could sit in the Spirit of Vancouver section. And for those willing to shell out $250, they'd actually get their name on the car—real small, of course, like teeny tiny, but it was still their name on a race car!

Obviously, $25, $100, and $250 increments weren't going to cover the full cost—at least not on the timeline we were working with— so we pursued larger sponsors as well. Our first big one came from Shell through a guy named Ed Theobald, who later worked with me in developing Electra Meccanica. Ed also introduced us to Pepsi and they gave us another big chunk of cash. We pieced the rest together from the odd local company here and there, and finally a few Spirit of Vancouver founders had to step up to the plate and contribute finishing funds, lest all our fundraising be for naught. We ended up getting our guy into the race just by the skin of our teeth.

With the full $110,000 raised, we were able to send our driver, Ross Bentley, to Indianapolis to test for his IndyCar license. Then we took the rest of the money and poured it into the gear and entrance fees for all three days of the race. How thrilled we were that we pulled it off. It was the beginning of a whole new life for me.

The excitement did, however, come with rose-coloured glasses. I had so much passion, I could raise funds for just about anybody. This wasn't a *bad* thing, of course, but my own talent and enthusiasm did distract me from being discerning. At the beginning of my career in car racing, I got caught up in my own ability to get the job done and couldn't see that the client I was raising money for was not the actual superstar I imagined him to be. At the time, I believed that anybody who worked and tried hard enough could become a champion.

I believed this so much that the only reason I could find for my client losing all the time was that he didn't have the most high-end equipment. A few years in, with two cars on our team and the other guy going quite a bit faster than my client, I couldn't understand why we weren't keeping up. I remember looking at the equipment, not really knowing the difference between this piece or that piece, but certain that the equipment was at the root of my client falling behind. I asked one of the crew guys, "What do we need here to make my guy as fast as the other guy?" I told him that I could raise more money to get him the right stuff—a flux capacitor, or whatever magical tool it was that we needed in order to win.

The crew guy just gave me the most horrified expression, like pure disbelief. I looked at him, mouth agape, still not getting it and not knowing what to say. He laughed a little, shook his head, and then explained to me gently that while my client was a very nice person, the other guy on the team was championship material. Then he just shut up and let the rest hang in the air.

That's when it clicked. It was the politest way he could say, "It's not the equipment." I looked back at the last three years and realized that we could take the exact same equipment, no flux capacitor, no magic engine, and put a different driver—one with championship material—in there and receive very different results.

I think the lesson here, in life and in business, is that it's nice to have your favourites and to support them, but you have to be open and flexible enough to recognize when you don't have the right people in the right places. Sometimes passion and hard work aren't enough. Watching too many Disney movies probably shaped those false beliefs in me. When lovable Herbie, the good fellow with big dreams, gets his lucky break, you start believing that anyone can do it. But that's not the way it works in real life. In real life you have to surround yourself with people who are actually capable of getting the job done—not just people who *think* they can get the job done.

Once I saw the truth, I couldn't unsee it. And it turned out that everybody on the team had understood the reality except for me, but nobody had the heart to come out and say, "Oh, that guy's having a fun time driving the car, but he's not a champion." Meanwhile, I'd genuinely believed that we could win the Indy 500, that all we needed was a lucky break and some magical equipment. Nope.

I look back at those first few years as an IndyCar agent and go, *How sweet was I in thinking that? So naive and adorable.* But you can't beat yourself up over the things you don't know. You learn as you go, you keep moving forward, and you don't forget those lessons. The next time you're faced with the same challenge in a different situation, you remember what you learned, and you act differently. The business of motorsports, like all businesses, gets a lot easier when you put the right person in the driver's seat.

As I was coming to this realization, the Spirit of Vancouver was falling apart. There was a lot of bad blood—former friends suing each other and so on. Not a good vibe. The timing however, being fortuitous as it always is, lined up perfectly for me to strike out on my own. We were in Indianapolis, and I was still working with the no-magical-equipment-is-going-to-fix-this client. There was no way he was going to qualify for the championship, but I was still getting him funding and sponsorships as if he was brilliant, because that was my job. Then one day, this short, blue-eyed guy came walking into the garage, reached out his hand, and said, "Hi, I'm Scott Sharp, and my sponsor says that if you can raise money for that guy, you can raise money for anybody. I want to drive IndyCar and I want to work with you."

At the time, I had no idea who he was, but I could see that he was a very charming young man. He was racing Camaros in the Trans-Am Series, and there's no way a guy driving a Camaro should drive IndyCar, but he was hell-bent on doing it—*and* he was good at it. So I went, "Sure. Why not?" I could tell he was easily already miles ahead of the guy I was working with, so I figured I'd give it a shot.

Scott Sharp became the first driver I signed to my own company, Ascend Sports Management, and as it turned out, signing him came with a lot of perks—including the good fortune of spending time with his godfather, Paul Newman. How cool is that? It was a real delight meeting and spending time with the man, the myth, the legend. And I was thrilled to discover that Paul Newman was just a regular guy. Like, the *most* regular guy. I think a lot of us assume that celebrities live in a different world, so it's a bit of a shocker to find out that not only do they live in the exact same world as us, but they're also just normal people. Meeting Paul Newman was a bit like if you met Barack Obama and he suggested you go to the Salvation Army to pick up some slacks and t-shirts or something. You'd be going, *I thought we were going fly in a private jet!* A bit of a shock to the system. But he was lovely guy and just about as kooky about motorsports as anybody I've ever seen.

After signing Scott, it wasn't long before I was working with drivers like Buddy Lazier, Scott Dixon, and other really talented drivers who were all a complete pleasure to support and assist on their journeys. As I started working with these clients who had real potential to win IndyCar championships and Indy 500s, the actual act of winning took some getting used to.

In 1994, I was representing Dominic Dobson at the Michigan 500 in Brooklyn, Michigan, which is a five-hundred-mile race on this big oval track and, completely out of nowhere, he finished third place. We were a new team, and his win completely blew us away. It hadn't even occurred to us before the race that we should figure out where the podium was because we had no expectations of placing. Once we'd collected ourselves after the race, none of us knew where to find the podium for the award ceremony. After that, I started to expect more and prepare accordingly.

Before I knew it, my career was taking off and I was jetting off to Detroit and Australia and Florida. Some mornings I still had to pinch myself when I woke up. I had long dreamt of travelling the world attending IndyCar races, but it always seemed out of reach. But now! Now, not only was I getting paid to be there, but drivers were actually seeking me out, flying me to races, and I was meeting Mario Andretti and Emerson Fittipaldi and shaking hands with David Letterman and James Garner. Even Roger Penske himself gave me the head nod of recognition in the green room. (I don't think he had any clue who I was, but just to be part of the recognizable furniture around the racetrack to legend Roger Penske … I mean, come on, my inner child had never been happier.) It's amazing how quickly you can burst into that stratosphere. And it all happened because I was so fired up about the work.

My job was to get drivers their sponsorships, and I was pretty damn good at it. I could go up to literally any company and say, "How would you like to have your name on a race car?"

And they'd go, "Are you kidding me?"

To which I would say, "No! I'm dead serious. You give us $10,000 and I'll put your name on a car, give you two trackside tickets, and you can come meet the driver and the team owner."

Their response was always something along of the lines of, "Shut up. Where do I sign?" And then, if the chemistry aligned, the next thing you know it would turn into a multimillion-dollar deal. It worked because I wasn't faking it. My enthusiasm was real and contagious. It's easy to get companies to sponsor you when you're passionate about what you're doing. Honestly, people would just throw money at me.

I'd always sweeten the deal with personal touches. We'd bring the drivers out for meet-and-greets, have them come to the shop and drink a coffee, eat an ice cream, wear the clothes, or do whatever was appropriate. We'd park the race car in front of their shop and make little mini cars with the company's logo on them to hand out, and then we'd take pictures and film the whole thing. Everyone would just be in awe.

I got good at making all different kinds of deals. Some companies would donate product instead of giving money. I knew the people who owned Rain X, this liquid you squeeze on your windshield to deflect water when it rains. I approached them for a sponsorship, and they offered me $250,000 worth of their product. But what am I going to do with $250,000 of windshield rain deflector?

So, I called up the Jim Pattison Group (one of the biggest companies in Canada) and they agreed to buy it off me—for a great deal—to put in Save-On-Foods or one of their other grocery stores. That's the sort of brokerage trade I learned from the flower business. Everybody's happy, and I got my driver the funds they needed to succeed.

I worked hard, but it was so joyful it didn't feel like hard work. It felt like a real honour to be part of the team and to get to hang out around those cars—such spectacular cars.

However, there was also a dark side to car racing. Think about your chances of dying in hockey or baseball. Pretty low, right? But in car racing? When I first heard that Hemingway quote, "There are three sports in the world: bullfighting, mountain climbing, and car racing. Everything else is a game," I thought, *Man, that's exactly right.* Mountain climbing is not for me. And bullfighting? Bullfighting is about as politically correct as horse racing. (I did dip my toes into horse racing at one point. I owned a horse through a syndicate and almost immediately regretted it. I kept asking people what happened to the horse if it didn't win, and nobody would answer me.) The risk is part of what makes the sport of car racing so enthralling. It's pure adrenaline and the highest stakes. But the enjoyment of the sport overall is never worth the loss.

I lost friends. I watched families lose their sons and their fathers. That was more horrific than I can tell you. I still think back to my time with Greg Moore, who was just a young man in Indy Lights when I was working with him. He had so much promise and potential when he got into IndyCar. He could have been racing still, with multiple championships and all that. His family lost a loved one, and the world lost a champion.

Car racing is life and death. I think that's why I've never felt called to become a professional racer myself. I love to drive, but I don't love to risk my life. I'm pretty decent at the sport—I've even won a Formula Enterprises Regional Championship—and I've been fortunate enough to race some beautiful cars, but if I ever start scaring myself on the track, I immediately slow down. If I see the other racers crowding ahead, I don't try to shoot up the middle of them in the hopes of winning the race. I let them sort themselves out. My number one rule when I drive is not to win, but to get back safe. To get back safe and to watch out for everyone else. Ultimately, I don't care if I come in last as long as I'm having a fun time. And I always trust my gut to guide me.

It's important to listen to your intuition in these high intensity situations—not just on the track but leading up to a race as well. I can think of more than one tragic racing death that occurred after a buildup of smaller injuries and incidents. Sometimes you can sense things going wrong, or maybe you notice your sense of balance is off. Those feelings can be signs that you need to consider stepping back. That might be your body's way of telling you to take a break—that it's time to stop what you're doing and go home. You can refresh and come back another day, as opposed to just pushing through. It takes a really bold person with a lot of integrity to do that. Like when Olympic gymnast Simone Biles walked away from competition and called it her "biggest win" yet. You have to do what's best for you and what's in the best interest of your health. It's never worth risking your life, even if your life isn't on the line. Say for example you planned a trip or started a business, and now something's telling you that it's not the right thing, that you need to step away. It's important that you listen to that feeling. No matter what anyone around you is telling you or pushing you to do, you have to trust your own gut first and foremost.

The race car industry can be harmful and wasteful in other ways too. One year we spent $12 million, and all we had to show for it was smashed car parts. I remember walking through the shop in Indianapolis one night by myself, this big garage full of worn-out tires, twisted metal, and destroyed engines, thinking, *Wow. There's got to be a better way of doing things.* For that kind of money, we could have built a library, a hospital, a school, or something that left an actual legacy. Instead, my team placed twentieth and twenty-second out of thirty-two cars. What's the point of that? I began to realize that I didn't want to contribute to the waste anymore.

That was another epiphany moment for me, one where I'd been carrying on with business as usual and all of a sudden something clicked. I asked myself, *What's truly going to matter fifty years from now? Is anyone going to care about what you did?* And, more importantly, *Am I going to care about what I did?*

My eyes stayed open after that moment. Awareness around the danger of fossil fuels was growing, and I started looking at the industry with a sharper perspective. While IndyCar was using methanol, a grain-based fuel, to run their cars (which is better than gasoline or diesel, both in terms of emissions and also safety because it has a higher flashpoint, meaning it has to get much hotter than other types of gas before it catches fire), it still wasn't sustainable for the planet. I knew we could do better. I knew we *had* to do better.

After several years, the glamour of the driving world began to fade. I remember waking up in Milwaukee sometime around 1997, the Monday after a race, and realizing that I was done. It was like Forrest Gump when he's running and running and running and all of a sudden goes, "I'm through running. I just want to go home."

For a while, I got completely caught up in the lifestyle. It was a whirlwind: fun until it wasn't, fulfilling until it was empty. And all of a sudden it was too much fast food, too much travel, and too many cheap hotels. The novelty had worn off. I was ready for change again. The desire to do something with purpose, something that would leave a legacy and help the world, carried me back home.

HEMPTOWN

You never change things by fighting the existing reality. To change something, build a new model that makes the existing model obsolete.

Buckminster Fuller

I had one of my first environmental wakeup calls while I was running the frozen yogourt franchise. We were prepping for a new marketing push and had just ordered $100,000 worth of beautiful, colourful Styrofoam cups when the news broke that CFCs were burning a hole in the ozone layer. CFCs, or chlorofluorocarbons, were in wide use in refrigeration, air conditioning, and aerosol spray cans like hairspray, and they were the chemical component used to expand polystyrene to create Styrofoam. Humans had invented a technology they thought was useful, but over time we discovered that it was actually incredibly harmful for the planet.

As environmental groups spread the messaging that polystyrene products had to go, mothers marched their kids in front of McDonald's franchises to demand an end to foam containers. This was the first time I truly connected the dots between human activity and climate degradation, and it was the beginning of my journey to being aggressively proactive. I learned the hard way that if you're not aware and on top of sustainability, it will come back to bite you in the behind. Because when the yogourt franchise decided to replace the foam cups with paper cups, we hit an eighteen-month waitlist. Everyone was making the switch at the same time, so we were stuck with cups that hurt the ozone *and* we lost the business of the clientele who were aware of and cared about the impacts of Styrofoam.

That experience stayed with me throughout my time working the race car circuit. It planted the seed in the back of my mind: What does it mean to plan for the future?

Sure, you can sit in your gas car and go, "We've driven gas cars forever, so me making the switch is not going to make that much of a difference," but you're lying to yourself. It really does make a difference. It's only once you're sweltering in a heat dome or your neighbourhood is drowning under a flood that you go, "Oh. I should have done more sooner."

I could have done more sooner too. While I was working the race car circuit, I wasn't thinking about the state of the world or the future of the planet. I was simply following my joy. But more and more along the way, I began to get curious, more engaged, and then I woke up to the reality that I have a role to play in fixing all of this.

I'd established myself and had enough clients in the industry that I could continue working in the IndyCar world without having to keep up the breakneck pace of the race car circuit. And now that I had some money of my own in my pocket, I felt ready to start a new business. I just had no idea what that business was going to be. I had a few thoughts swirling around my head, and I was keeping my eyes open, meeting with different people and companies, but nothing was clicking. Then one day, a fax came through my office. There was a local company, kind of like a Groupon thing (Groupon is an app for local deals around town), that would send out faxes regularly. On that day, the paper curling out of the machine was about a closing out sale for a place called Hemptown.

I was confused by what they were trying to sell. At the time, the only association I had with hemp was marijuana. It looked like they were selling clothes—there's nothing illegal about that—but it sure sounded naughty. I had a couple of friends go by and scope out their warehouse in Vancouver, and they reported back that Hemptown Clothing seemed like a reasonable business, so I decided to go in and check it out for myself. That's what an entrepreneur does, right? You have to investigate, poke and prod around until you find the right thing. Kind of like kissing a bunch of frogs before you find your prince.

I arrived at their shop and was immediately taken aback by their huge, erratic inventory. The warehouse was filled with odds and ends: kimonos, t-shirts, slacks, dresses. Everything you could imagine. The clothing was good quality, but it was all over the place. It was clear that they didn't have a strong business model, but the hemp products really intrigued me.

The owners, a young couple, came over and introduced themselves, and right away started giving me the spiel on hemp and how good it is for the environment—especially compared to the damaging production of cotton, the go-to fabric for the world. They told me how hemp grows naturally in cold climates where you don't have to irrigate, and how easily it can grow without any insecticides or pesticides. Cotton, meanwhile, is an incredibly water intensive crop and often utilizes dangerous chemicals. Globally, cotton covers 2.5% of the world's cultivated land, but cotton farmers use 4.7% of the world's pesticides and 10% of the world's insecticides (Pesticide Action Network UK). I knew from my background in horticulture just how dangerous and prevalent these chemicals could be, so hemp seemed like a no-brainer: a clear solution to a real problem. I decided I wanted to put my weight behind it.

My head, always in the race car mindset, went immediately to uniforms. I wasn't thinking yet about working with the company over the long-term; I just thought it would be a cute gag to dress the team up in hemp. I asked the Hemptown owners if doing race suits was something they'd be interested in and the guy's eyes lit up. He gasped and went, "Would I?!" Turns out he was a real car racing nut.

We had the whole team done up in hemp for a race in Cleveland, and the week before we arrived, I sent out a memo to all the newspapers in the area that there was going to be a team in all-hemp uniforms. The media went nuts. Our team was a midrange Indy Lights team, nothing really to write home about, but all of a sudden everybody was paying attention. We had all the newspapers reporting, "Oh wow, it's flame resistant," and, "It's great for the environment." The team owner and the whole race crew were blown away by all the press we received. The uniforms were a hit.

Hemptown had a great product, and the people running the company were fantastic when it came to understanding their products and their industry but, unfortunately, they didn't have the experience or discipline necessary to turn their ideas into a successful business. They'd given us the uniforms at no charge—which was a huge success for our team—but they made no money. This is fine sometimes for a company if the exposure is worth it, but they were not in a place to be giving anything away for free.

About eight months after we collaborated on the uniforms, I learned that the company was on the verge of going bankrupt. They couldn't make ends meet and were about to go under. If they'd been doing well on their own, I may not have been so incentivized to invest, but they were about to close up shop and I figured this company was too important to go broke. So I made them a pitch. I said, "Look, you're broke. I can tell you love the company, but you are struggling to put the right pieces in the right place. I can help. I'll refinance the business, capitalize it, and give the two of you one-third. You keep running the day-to-day operations, and I'll take care of the rest."

They agreed and we jumped in with both feet. I even bought them a car because they had no way to get around. I'm not made of money, but it felt important. I knew acquiring this company was a calculated risk that would pay off—not just for making money in the future, but for fighting the pollution of cotton and helping the planet. I decided to risk quite a bit of capital, and the owners were most grateful that their dream wasn't going to die.

The product was good, so that made the work easy. They already had quality material, solid designs, a healthy production line, and good relationships with buyers. All we needed was simplification. We couldn't do kimonos, t-shirts, dresses, and slacks in all these different sizes and colours. It was way too much, and inevitably we'd end up not having the right size or colour that the customer was looking for. So, I told them, "Listen up. We're going to make one thing, and we're going to make it right."

I call this the New York Fries method, where you do one thing and you do it exceptionally well. There is zero point in spending thousands of dollars on all different kinds of inventory if you're never going to sell half of it, right? That's unfocused. It's not good business.

They agreed to narrow it all down and we built up from there. To start, I suggested Oxford shirts: one colour, one size. We made a thousand of them. The shirts came in, we sold them all out, and then we made another round. Simple, straightforward, easy. It worked. The company got back on track—and quickly, too.

With the company relaunched, we had people coming in off the street saying they wanted to work for us for free—in sales, manufacturing, marketing. They understood how important this business was for the planet, and they offered to work with us to make the company successful. They were happy to wait to accept payment once there was enough money to go around. That's when the light bulb went off for me about mission-based businesses. It wasn't just the employees or the customers who were passionate and excited about what we were making, but also the suppliers and the investors and everybody involved. That's when I realized that our return on investment shouldn't just be cash—it should be something that's good for the planet. We had a mission to reduce the use of cotton, one of the world's most polluting crops, and everyone got behind it.

All that said, I still felt a little weird working with hemp because of its association with cannabis (keep in mind, this was nearly two decades before cannabis was legalized in Canada), so despite my excitement for the product, I was nervous to tell my parents about it. I was a young guy, and I thought they were going to be upset with me when they found out, maybe thinking I was running some sort of marijuana business. But when my mom came to visit the shop, she broke out into a huge smile and turned to me to say, "This is what I did as a little girl."

Turns out my mom worked in a hemp factory in Germany when she was a kid. Growing up, she would tell us about her time in the *hanf* factory. Whenever we complained about the hours in the greenhouse, she'd tell us stories about how her little fingers would get all bruised from doing the spinning day after day. But she never used the word "hemp" or "marijuana," just "*hanf.*" So when she discovered that I'd followed in her footsteps working with hemp, there was no confusion or judgment. She completely understood what we were doing, and she was thrilled to see me innovating in that industry.

We used the company's existing distribution infrastructure to sell our product to clothing shops across Canada and the States. After one round of orders would sell out, we'd do another one. Once the Oxford shirts were an established success, we did a line of t-shirts. Our suppliers were happy to pick up a second item after the success of the first. Meanwhile, to expand our product even further, I would reach out to businesses I knew would be aligned with our mission. We uniformed the waiters at the iconic Vancouver vegetarian restaurant, The Naam, and we sold product to Howard Schultz, CEO of Starbucks. He bought up a whole $100,000 worth of inventory. We also worked with legendary Nike and Adidas marketing whiz Peter Moore. Everybody was getting excited about hemp. Then, as the internet launched in a big way, we went online with the rest of the world and began marketing Hemptown even further.

Our product was a hemp and organic cotton blend—45% hemp, 55% cotton—that was imported from China. We wanted to do 100% hemp, but the material was just too rough. As you may know, straight hemp feels like horsehair or burlap. It's an incredibly strong material but incredibly uncomfortable to wear. When you mix it with half cotton, it improves the wearability. It's still not super soft, but it makes a significant improvement. After we brought the bulk fabric in from China, we manufactured the clothing at our workshop in Vancouver.

The long-term plan was to grow the hemp in Canada—to sow fields of hemp in the prairies, build a mill, and produce everything locally. As I began making inroads on that plan, building toward the goal of being completely sustainable, I received a call while sitting in my office at Venables and Clark in East Vancouver late one night. The phone rang with an Ottawa area code and I picked it up, said hello, and heard a voice on the other end ask, "Is this Hemptown?"

"Yes, you've reached Hemptown, and you're speaking to Jerry Kroll, the owner. Who am I talking to?"

The voice responded, "I'm Dr. Wing Sung, a scientist at the National Research Council." He proceeded to tell me that scientists at the National Research Council (NRC) had been working on a proprietary hemp fibre technology, a way of processing hemp to make it softer to wear, and that they were looking for a commercial partner.

He asked me, "Would you be interested in a proprietary fibre that is as smooth as silk or cotton but made of hemp?"

"Hell yes," I said, followed immediately by, "How did you get my number?"

He explained that he had been in a laboratory with a bunch of assistants talking about how they were going to commercialize the product when one of the assistants tugged at his shirt and said, "Hey, what about the shirt I'm wearing? It's from a company called Hemptown." They looked at the clothing tag and found our number—because I had very cleverly gotten our phone number and URL printed onto all of the tags. And that's when he'd called.

The NRC still had about $600,000 worth of work to do to finish the process. They asked us for half of the funding in exchange for the exclusive rights. Naturally, we agreed. I knew this would be a priceless investment for the company.

With our investment, the National Research Council was able to finish developing a cutting-edge, all-natural enzymatic process that would unlock the potential of hemp, resulting in a sustainable natural fibre as soft and durable as cotton, without the environmental risks.

You know what cotton feels like, but did you know that the softness of the cotton is based on the *staple length*? Not to be confused with thread count or weave, the staple length refers to the length of the fibres that make up the fluff of cotton known as the *boll*. The longer the staple length, the softer the cotton is. This means that items made with long staple cotton don't pill or tear as much and can even become softer over time. Normally, the length of cotton fibres is between half an inch and three-quarters of an inch. Our staple length was four feet long. When Dr. Sung sent me a sample of the hemp fibre, it was as soft as cotton.

I took it to my friend Peter Moore and he looked at me like I was levitating. We had already begun the process of taking Hemptown public, so the added value of this patent was gold. That made raising the (significant amount of) money needed to complete the process of going public much easier.

As we prepped to take Hemptown Clothing to market, I knew we had some changes to make. Today, if you called your company "Hemptown," you could sell it for a billion bucks, people wouldn't even need to know what you were doing. But back then, hemp wasn't hip; it still freaked people out. If you tried to call your public company "Hemptown," the market would laugh at you, and your stock wouldn't go up. So, in order to take us to the next level, I knew we needed a different name—something that evoked innovation, like Gore-Tex or rayon. I started brainstorming.

In Saskatchewan, in between Regina and Saskatoon, there is a town called Craik. Craik wanted to produce and process hemp for us. They even sold us eighty acres of land for $1. In honour of their generosity, I decided to brand Hemptown with a name that reflected them. My first idea was "Craylon," but then I realized it sounded too nylon-y. Next I was thinking "Crayler" or "Crailar." I looked them both up and "Crailar" was available, so we went with that and stylized it as CRAiLAR.

We changed the name and began the gruelling process of taking the company public. It is an incredibly challenging undertaking, so it was to my relief that the market was super receptive to our product. There was a ton of interest, not just because of the clothing we were selling, but because of the fabric we had developed with the NRC.

Unfortunately, at this point, things took a turn for the worse. A group of men with stock options started getting involved in the company. My team were all excited about these guys coming to the table and they urged me to listen to them—and I, after building this company for several years, was ready for something new.

So, I let them take over, which ended up meaning that I had to watch the company I carefully and painstakingly built get taken in a completely different direction than the one I'd planned out for it. I watched these new guys refuse to tap into CRAiLAR's true potential. I mean, you hadn't hear about CRAiLAR until you read this book, right? You're reading this chapter thinking, *I still wear cotton. Where's my soft, environmentally friendly hemp alternative?*

While the National Research Council had completed the development, the CRAiLAR fibre was never used while I was part of the company because we didn't have a system in place to produce it. The plan was to build a mill and produce it in Canada, but the new guys never got it done. They actually stopped producing clothing altogether in order to focus 100% on continuing to develop the product. I couldn't understand this—that was our bread and butter! When they shut down production, I asked them why they stopped selling shirts, and you know what they said to me? They told me to get lost because I wasn't "contributing" anymore.

That stung. So, I got lost. I sold my shares and hit the road.

CRAiLAR should have changed natural fabrics forever. That product should have been as big as Gore-Tex. It should have revolutionized hemp clothing the way Gore-Tex revolutionized waterproof fabric. Maybe it still will someday.

Hemp as a crop is still underutilized. It could be used for manufacturing fibreglass, paper and plastic products, and even oil for candles and paint. The only area where it seems to have been fully embraced is in the food industry as hemp milk and hemp seeds. Hilariously, back in 1998 when we started the company, people thought they would get high off of eating hemp bread or hemp granola. Today, people understand the difference between hemp products and cannabis products, but it's still a vastly untapped market.

Looking back, I realize I should have pushed back more. I had more shares than anybody and they desperately needed the oversight—this was a product that deserved the support and follow through. That was my fault at the time. I should have stayed involved and seen CRAiLAR through to ensure its success, but they were actively pushing me out and I didn't want to stay where I wasn't wanted. So, I packed a couple suitcases into the back of my Porsche, grabbed my dog Zuka, and off we went to California.

CALIFORNIA DREAMIN'

*Whether you think you can, or you
think you can't—you're right.*

Henry Ford

When the people who took over Hemptown told me my services weren't needed and that I should retire and go race cars in
California, I listened. Except for the retirement part. Despite a
handsome payout from the sale of CRAiLAR, I wasn't ready to
chill out and go out to seed. Sure, I could have spent the rest of my
days lazing around on a beach somewhere and racing cars for fun,
but I was too afraid that I'd wake up one day, twenty or thirty years
down the road, and the planet would be dead. And I would have
done absolutely nothing to help.

So, I committed to continuing to innovate and started spending all
my retirement money—I mean *all* of it, four million bucks, right
to zero—on building electric cars. At the end of the day, who cares
how much you have in the bank? I'd rather be broke and have tried
to do something about the state of the world than have millions of
dollars while the planet goes to hell.

Besides, innovating is way more fun than sitting on the beach.

There's no better way to develop an electric car than to start with
a race car. No regular person is going to drive their car as hard as

a race car driver, so if an electric car passes the race car test, it's tested; it's going to work well for everyone else. Those days all I could think about was building electric race cars. It had been on my mind since the early 1990s when I saw the busted up parts and went, "Hold on, we can do better than this gas thing." Really, it had been on my mind since I was eleven years old, playing with my Hot Wheels Sizzlers.

I had been going down to California often and was spending a lot of time with my young race car driving client, Duncan Ende, and his mom, Karen. Karen was a delightful lady, surely one of the most interesting people I've ever met. She was a book collector and knew something about everything. Her son wanted to become a race car driver, so we bonded naturally. Karen and I spoke often about my goals and aspirations to develop electric race cars, and one day she told me that she wanted me to meet her friend Tim Collins. She knew he was interested in all the same things, and she figured we'd get along well and that we could maybe even work together.

Tim was an investment banker from the San Francisco area. He was a big, gregarious guy with a big, outgoing personality. He had a real positive outlook on life and always had a smile on his face. Karen gave him the rundown of who I was and what I was about, so the first thing he said to me when we met was, "Do you want to go car racing?"

I looked at him and said, "Well, to tell you the truth, what I'd really like to do is build electric race cars."

And he just about dropped to the floor. "That's exactly what I was thinking," he said. "How would you like to work together?"

That was the beginning of KleenSpeed Technologies. It was yet another one of those magical moments where the right person shows up at the right time. By putting my intentions out there, talking to Karen about my dreams, I created the space for everything to line up.

I'd always wanted to live in San Francisco because it's a lovely place to be, but it turns out there's not much room in the city for tinkering. In its place, I chose Morgan Hill, which is about an hour-and-a-half drive south of San Francisco, just below San Jose, where there was ample garage space available. Morgan Hill is a small, clean, and friendly California town. It's also incredibly hot because it's inland, so it regularly gets to over one hundred degrees (which is brutal weather for this Canadian). I found this little compound where I could rent a place to live and a car garage to build in and got straight to work. I found some racing mechanics who were keen to help on the project, and we started sourcing the best parts to build one of the world's first electric race cars.

My job was to build the cars, while Tim's job was to raise the money. Two of the first people Tim introduced me to were his friends Martin Eberhard and Marc Tarpenning. They were also working on building electric cars—not race cars like us, but electric cars for regular people—so we had a lot to talk about. While Tim's job was supposed to be finding us financing, he didn't introduce me to Martin and Marc because they had any money to offer us. In fact, they asked *me* if I would give them money to help fund their company—a company called Tesla. The first time Tim and I met Martin and Marc was at a place called Bucks. Bucks is a famous venture capital cafe in Woodside, about halfway between San Francisco and San Jose. Every day, that place was packed with young people with ideas and laptops, and older people with money—thousands of start-ups have been brought to life over breakfast there. We had a good time chatting with Martin and Marc and went to check out their shop. We ended up meeting several times after that, having breakfast, catching each other up on what the other one was doing, and hashing through all the difficulties of innovating something completely new.

While Tim went around socializing with folks to raise funds, I got to work on building the cars. We bought a couple of pre-owned sports racer cars, a Stohr and a West, to use as the base—what is called the *chassis*—and stripped away all the unnecessary parts. Both of those cars are lightweight, chain-driven cars with high performance motorcycle motors. The motor drives the chain, and if you've got half a brain, you realize you can take the motorcycle motor out and put an electric motor in, because all you're doing is spinning a chain. There's no drama to it. Next, all you have to do is figure out where to put the motor controller and the batteries—there were side pods we could place them in. Once it's all connected, you press the accelerator pedal and everything goes. I didn't even hire any mechanics, though I was fortunate that right next to where I'd set up shop in this little compound there was a race shop with mechanics working on their own stuff, so whenever they had time or something new arrived, they would come over, wrench on the cars, and help bolt it all together.

I placed an order for the best electric motor and drive system and electric batteries available at the time, and it wasn't long before we had the cars all open and ready to go, sprockets and chains and everything in place. Then it was just a waiting game for the motor and drive system to arrive. I ordered it from the go-to electric car motor guy at the time, thinking we'd be off to the races in no time. But the products took forever to arrive. After ordering the motor and drive system, this fellow promised us we'd get them in three weeks. And then three weeks turned into three months, and three months into six months, and so on, until finally I had to call him up and light a fire to get things moving.

The batteries we used were 400-volt lithium-ion batteries that cost about $40,000. That was the best product you could get your hands on at the time. Everything was expensive. Nobody really knew what they were doing. The whole industry was in its infancy. And there were so many delays. But it was all worth it.

We tinkered away on the cars for about a year, trial and error-ing our way through, until one day we got a call from NASA. Certainly one of the cooler phone calls I've received in my entire life. NASA!

I'd met several other people during my time in Morgan Hill who were interested in electric drive systems and, as luck would have it, these people knew people at the NASA Research Park at Moffett Field in Mountain View. They got a hold of me through a friend and said they were interested in the work we were doing. They invited us to relocate and work on site at the Research Park.

We packed up and moved shop to Mountain View, a forty-minute drive away and, delightfully, right on the water. It was a literal breath of fresh air—the temperature went from 110 degrees down to 75 degrees—and I couldn't have been more excited to be there. Instead of being in an industrial park, we were now building our cars in one of the coolest, most mysterious environments imaginable. We even had our own racetrack right outside the workshop door!

Working there at the NASA Research Park was like being in an episode of *The X-Files*. Every day you'd go in and there'd be an armed guard checking your ID and waving you through. We'd be out on the runway, testing our car in between fighter jets and presidential planes, and we'd come off the runway as Martin and Marc were heading out to test the very first version of the Tesla.

The NASA folks were incredibly encouraging. They rented the space to us, this huge building, for a nominal fee. This was way before the general public was excited about electric cars, but they saw and understood the potential. They knew electric cars were the future and that innovators needed support to bring that future toward us faster.

Something that not everyone knows is that while electric cars are the future, they are also a part of the past. Electric cars have actually been around as long as gas cars—in fact, in 1900, 38% of the cars on the road in the US were electric—but they didn't become a sustainably viable technology until battery management systems were invented. The first electric batteries were lead acid. They weighed a ton and had a range of about fifty kilometres (which was fine because back then you were just using horse roads). At the time, lead acid battery–run cars were actually easier to use than gas cars because in order to start the gas car, you needed to get up front and hand crank the engine. It was a violent operation that took a lot of strength and if it ever kicked back, you could break your arm. With the electric battery car however, all you had to do was press a button to start it. No risk of broken bones. Well, as long as the batteries didn't explode on you.

Once someone invented something called the electric starter, it solved the gas car's internal combustion engine hand crank problem. Now all you had to do was press a button or turn a key to go. That's what killed the electric car the first time, back at the turn of the century. Gas cars were just as easy to use as electric cars but there was no risk of exploding batteries.

What's allowing for the death of the gas car today is not just the improvement of electric batteries themselves—though that's a huge factor—but also electric battery management systems (BMS), computer systems that monitor the batteries and regulate the usage and charging of those batteries. The BMS is what talks to every single one of the battery cells, making sure they stay in balance—in sync—and regulated. Because when they're not in sync, the batteries can fail, and if the system gets confused and ends up charging a full battery instead of a half-full battery, or doesn't discharge from the battery once it is full, the batteries will go *BOOM*.

The first BMS that came out was massive, about the size of a saxophone case, but now they've been innovated down to about the size of a shoebox. That's what really killed the gas car—not the motor, not the batteries themselves, and not even Elon Musk, but battery management systems. Now we can use inexpensive lithium-ion batteries and control them properly with near-zero risk. Since it's been perfected, you can now plug in any electric car mindlessly to charge up to 1,600 kilometres per hour with no fear of the batteries breaking. You can fill up your car with electric power and, just like that, take off for a long drive. There's not an internal combustion motor that can keep up with this technology.

Back in 2006, when I first started building electric cars, the battery management systems were still being developed. We all know that there's a big difference between something being invented and something being perfected, and the BMS definitely wasn't perfected yet. It was the primitive days of its development, which meant that it took forever to charge the batteries and they would often get out of balance, or worse.

One day at the NASA Research Park, I was driving the car around on a skid pad in the parking lot, just to put some mileage on it, and I heard this *pop, pop, pop*. I can still remember the smell in the air and going, "What the hell is that?" before it clicked: it was the batteries blowing up. I have to say, it was my least favourite way to spend forty grand. (Maybe now you're starting to understand how easily I could spend all my "retirement" money.)

It's all part and parcel of innovating a new technology, of course. You trial and error, error and trial, until one day, it finally works out. The Wright brothers never had a successful flight before Kitty Hawk. Once you have a successful flight, you can repeat and adjust from there, but until you get there, it's all exploding batteries and troubleshooting and hand-wringing, pressing on forward and holding the vision.

In this scenario, the failure was due to immature technology—batteries and a battery management system that just weren't there yet. You just have to accept the loss and acknowledge that you're part of the process of progress.

There's always options in regard to where and from whom you choose to order your products, but as rough as that system was then, the other systems available at the time didn't have the same performance abilities. We paid a pretty penny for those exploding batteries, but we wanted the best of the best. It didn't matter the cost. I doubt the Wright brothers worried about how much the propellers cost. They just got the best stuff available because they were trying to fly a freaking plane for the first time. If you don't buy the top tier equipment, you're not giving yourself a fair shot. You don't say, "Well, let's save some money and go for this second-rate motor," or whatever. That's never going to work. Do your research and invest in the best.

The mechanics who were helping me put the race car together were more into car customization than anything else, so at a certain point I brought in some engineers to refine the process. The mechanics had done a lot of things that didn't make sense. They were good guys, they just didn't know any better. When I brought in the engineering students, they went, "This is set up all wrong; you've got to do this and that and this …" They tweaked the car and made changes, and things actually started to work.

You always bring in engineering because you can always improve products. You're always adding engineers, adding ideas, refining the product. It can feel like a never-ending cycle.

Once everything was in place and working, it was time to debut the car. The first time we debuted a workable version was at the Sports Car Club of America at Laguna Seca. We wanted to show them what we were doing because we wanted to run demonstrations the following year. I couldn't wait to see their reactions. I figured it would go well, but I still had nerves.

On the debut day, we totally blew everyone away. They were shocked. I remember one of the guys looking at me, slack-jawed, going, "Holy crap, you built an electric race car?!" The Sports Car Club of America PR and media people were taking pictures. We ended up in their magazines with the headline stating that we were the "look of things to come."

The following year, we brought our car to Laguna Seca's electric showcase. Everybody had showed up with electric bikes, motorcycles, and cars—our car was the real standout. It kicked all the other cars' butts! We set records for fastest electric race car at both Laguna Seca and Sears Point that year.

Once we got a new version of our car finished—a brand new shiny electric race car—that's when we did a proper reception. Marc and Martin and a whole bunch of other people came over to the NASA Research Park and we drove the car out in front of everyone. It was a beautiful sunny day in Mountain View. Everyone was thrilled. It felt so exciting, like we were starting to move forward in a big way, but that's when my business partner said, "We're not going to show anybody else our car until it's faster than every gas car out there."

Why he thought it was a good idea to keep our innovation in a vacuum, I'll never know. As if a bunch of electric vehicle guys sitting around a small racetrack in California congratulating each other is going to change the industry. Can you imagine what would have happened if we took the car out to the Petit Le Mans race in Atlanta to properly show it off? Now that would have attracted some investment! If we showed up amongst the Porsches and Toyotas and Mercedes and Ferraris and made them stop practice for twenty minutes so we could take our electric car for a spin around the track, everybody would go, "Oh my God. *That* is an electric car?!" That would have gotten us noticed, that would have gotten us funding, that would have launched us into the stratosphere. Even if we had driven the car at thirty miles an hour, we would have gotten so much money from people seeing its potential. By the time our car became the fastest car on the track, we wouldn't need any more money. The innovation would have already been done.

That made me realize it was time for a business divorce. You don't keep your best ideas secret. No! You start building interest from day one—telling the story, amplifying it to media and funders and marketers. Stealth mode start-ups rarely take off.

So, in 2010, I made Tim an offer. I said, "Look. This isn't working. We can split the company fifty-fifty and go our separate ways, or you can buy me out for the same deal."

He thought it over and told me he wanted to keep going with the company. So, I let him buy me out. KleenSpeed Technologies became all his, and I decided to return to Vancouver. It would have been a disappointment, except for the fact that I knew exactly what I was going to do next.

THINKING SOLO

We choose to go to the moon, not because
it is easy, but because it is hard.

John F. Kennedy

Every Saturday morning in the late 1980s, my running group would jog around False Creek, an industrial and residential neighbourhood on the edge of the ocean inlet in Vancouver, and every week we would pass this little wooden shop on the corner of 1st Avenue and Quebec Street. The shop had a glass window, and next to the window was a table. As we ran by, the contents of the table always caught my eye.

On that table were manuals and books from Italy laid out: Porsche and Alfa Romeo books from the 1950s, '60s, and '70s, as well as drawings and sketches of classic cars and manuals on how to build them. They were yellow and curling with age, piled haphazardly on the table. Every Saturday morning, I would pause my run to press my nose up against the glass and get a better look at the materials. It was like jogging by Leonardo da Vinci's studio and seeing his pencil and engineering drawings lying around or passing by somebody's home and seeing a Gordie Howe rookie card just sitting there out on the coffee table. I thought to myself, *This is incredible. I need to get in there and meet these people.*

When I wandered into Intermeccanica for the first time, I found a dark and dingy workshop, like an old wooden barn. It was pure romance—everything I'd been dreaming of my whole life—even before I charged up those Hot Wheels Sizzlers or had my first visit to the racetrack. I'd been dreaming of being around—and building—beautiful cars since the day I went to the theatre and watched *The Love Bug* for the first time.

It was at that movie theatre on Columbia Street in New Westminster that my lifelong obsession with car racing began. I was seven years old when my parents took me. The cars zooming around the track, whipping back and forth nearly crashing into and bashing up against each other got my adrenaline pumping and captured my imagination like nothing had before. But it wasn't Herbie that made me fall in love with cars. Herbie was, of course, very lovable, and the clear hero of the film. The car that caught my attention was the villain of the film: a sleek yellow sports car with a black racing stripe down the middle. That's who I wanted to root for. I knew it was wrong—I knew Herbie was the one I was supposed to be cheering for, and I did feel guilty about it. But his nemesis was *way* cooler. I had no choice but to root for the bad guy.

As fate would have it, Herbie's nemesis, that charismatic yellow sports car, was an Intermeccanica Apollo—a 1965 sports car with an Italian body and an American V8 under the hood built with love by the company I would acquire four-and-a-half decades later. It wasn't until years after I'd befriended and developed a relationship with the owners—Frank, Paula, and their son, Henry—that I realized they were the people responsible for the car of my childhood dreams. I had no idea as I was jogging by that these were the brilliant innovators whose hands, hearts, and minds had created the car that inspired me to make my own cars.

If you told me when I was seven years old at the movies that the yellow car Herbie was racing against had been made by the company I was going to own one day, you would have blown my adolescent mind. Today, I can't help but to lean into the belief of karma or fate with a synchronicity like that, but at the time I was jogging by, all I knew was that I was being drawn in.

Founded in Turin, Italy in 1959 by Frank and Paula Reisner, Intermeccanica was an automobile manufacturer specializing in unique craft sports cars. They began by selling specialized exhaust systems and other auto parts, slowly and methodically building their Intermeccanica legacy. At the time, Turin was the hub of the specialty automotive world. With a rich history of metal casting, born out of medieval armour, car builders from around the world congregated to develop their skills and follow their passions. Anything could be done in Turin when it came to sports cars, and the more unique, the better.

While everyone else was modifying existing car bodies, Frank brought a special twist and a new way of doing things to the table. He would build the chassis from the ground up, import American auto parts, and place the existing bodies on top of them. Intermeccanica cars were sleek and stylish but never extravagant. Their mission had always been quality and value. No unnecessary bells and whistles. Just a solid, attractive product. Part of their charm was focusing on doing things that other people would find too difficult. When I asked Frank and Paula's son Henry, my eventual business partner, about his parents' legacy, he told me, "If you do the things that nobody else can do and you do it well, nobody else is going to be smarter or better or faster."

In the early days, I'd drop by the Intermeccanica shop on 1st and Quebec once or twice a year, just to see what they were doing and offer my respects. Frank and his team were always building cars—mainly Porsche 356 replicas—and they weren't just fixing or assembling car kits. They were building the cars from the ground up: designing, engineering, and fabricating magnificent sports cars, right then and there. They'd tolerate me poking around and asking questions and fawning over their legacy (I treated them like the legends they are), and they were never unfriendly. In fact, they were delightful, charming people. They appreciated just how much enthusiasm I had for the cars, and they could see that my visits weren't me just trying to get a cheap deal. I just loved being in the presence of their greatness.

Over the years, our relationship developed, and Frank told me about his attempts to build an electric car. In the 1990s, he investigated what it would take to make a Speedster electric, drawing up logistical plans while Paula crunched the numbers. It was early days, so lead acid batteries were the only batteries available, and they were very large and very heavy. There was a possibility of pulling an electric car off—Frank succeeded with a design that would have fit the batteries into the car—however, the performance would have dropped so far, he decided that there was no point in pursuing it.

Sadly, Frank passed away at the turn of the twenty-first century. He worked all the way up until the week he died. For him, with Intermeccanica, there was no separation between life, love, and work. After Frank passed, Henry came out of the woodwork and started chatting me up when I came in for visits. Before he'd just be tinkering away in the background, not engaging or saying hi. Once we got to talking, Henry told me he was interested in the idea of going electric and that he wanted to keep a friendly conversation open about the potential of working together one day.

The first idea Henry and I discussed was electrifying the Porsche 356. That never came to fruition because it's very difficult to get the electric systems together for the Porsche—it still is—and, while we bounced some other ideas around, nothing clicked. Then I went off to California to develop KleenSpeed and build electric race cars. But as much fun as I was having innovating down in California, Intermeccanica was never far from my mind. And neither was the Corbin Sparrow, the first one-seater car I'd ever laid eyes on.

I first came across the Corbin Sparrow in 1999 at the Pebble Beach Concours d'Elegance in, you guessed it, Pebble Beach, California. The Concours d'Elegance is an automotive event that takes place every August and celebrates two hundred of the most prized collector cars in the world. There was a buzz going around the event about this one-seater car called the Corbin Sparrow. I kept hearing about it from different people, so I went to have a look.

Immediately upon laying eyes on it, I knew it was something special. Like nothing I'd ever seen before, it hit me all at once—the efficiency and the function of a one-seater electric car. It made perfect sense. This was the transportation solution we didn't know we needed. It struck me as I stood there: this little jelly bean of a car would completely change the game. A year later, I bought the rights to sell them in Canada.

But I never got the opportunity to sell the Corbin Sparrow in Canada—though I did import one for myself to drive around Vancouver, much to the chagrin and confusion of the local authorities. The Sparrow's makers, Corbin Motors, filed for bankruptcy three years later after building less than three hundred Sparrows. Nevertheless, I kept in touch with them over the years and never stopped believing in the potential of a one-seater electric car. As I was wrapping up KleenSpeed and making my way back to Vancouver, I laid all my ideas out in my head. I figured I knew exactly what I wanted to do, where I wanted to go, and who

I wanted to do it with. I knew it was finally time to work with Intermeccanica to develop a one-seater electric car.

I arrived back in Canada as my Fisker Karma was being delivered. Just six months earlier, my parents had told me that they "wouldn't see electric cars in their lifetime," and now, not only was I driving an electric car, but I was driving a strong, sexy, gorgeous beast of an electric car.

The Fisker Karma was the first true electric sports car. It is a car that announces itself, a car that takes up space. The Fisker Karma is the car that paved the way for Tesla and showed everyone what electric cars were capable of. Sure, there was the Prius and the Leaf which were both very significant cars, but they were not fancy or particularly attractive. You didn't have anything sleek, sexy, or muscular—what you truly needed to be successful—until the Karma's arrival. It was a big deal to be driving this car.

For the launch of the Karma, they did a run of one hundred and called it the "Founders Series." Henrik Fisker himself signed the dash. The first car went to Leonardo DiCaprio, the second to Al Gore, the third one to Colin Powell, the fourth to Prince Albert of Monaco, the fifth to a member of the royal family in Denmark, and the sixth went to little ol' me. I always thought it was a huge honour to be the first "nobody" to get their hands on one. The second my Karma arrived, I powered it up and drove down to the Intermeccanica shop at 1st and Quebec and said to Henry, "Get in, buddy, I'm going to show you what an electric car can be."

Henry was jazzed when he saw the car (though not as jazzed as me, because that was simply not possible) and even more jazzed when he experienced the ride. Not only does the Fisker Karma run smooth, but it's also super-fast too. Honestly, it's impossible not to be impressed with that vehicle. Truly, it is one of the most luxurious vehicles ever built. It will always be a marquee car.

As we drove around, I filled Henry in on all the innovators and visionaries I'd met in California, including one of the engineers behind the Fisker Karma, a woman who was now working for Tesla. I told him about the last days of KleenSpeed, including my frustrations with Tim and how important it was to me now to have a business partner with the same clear goals as me. And then I told him that Mike Corbin had been in touch because he wanted to work on a second-generation Sparrow. I suggested that we might buy the manufacturing rights and build Sparrows here in Vancouver.

Henry was super interested in this prospect, especially as business at Intermeccanica was still slow after the 2008 financial collapse. So, I flew us down to California to check out the Corbin workshop. After touching down, the first thing we did was visit my friend at the Tesla gigafactory in Fremont, California—the original gigafactory, a massive facility clocking in at 5.5 million square feet—and my friend snuck us in and gave us a tour of the place so Henry could see all the ins and outs first-hand. They had no idea who we were as we walked around, checking out all the battery packs and prototypes and cars being built.

Next, we went to visit the Corbin Sparrow guys, a father and son duo. We were really excited to see what they were dreaming up and to hear more about the potential of working together, but as we toured the massive workshop where they were running a successful automotive seat business (remember the original Sparrow flunked in 2003), we saw no sign of second-generation Sparrow production. As it turned out, they hadn't done any work to improve the Sparrow since the last time I'd been in communication with them and we could see real acrimony between father and son. As we toured the shop, looking at what they were doing (or rather, what they weren't doing), Henry shot me glances like, *What is going on here?* It became obvious to me at that point in time that we weren't going to be able to work with them, and that the Sparrow was caput all over again. When we left the facility, Henry and I looked at each other and just shook our heads.

After a bit more touring around, we got on an airplane and flew back. It felt like a real disappointment. How many years had I been dreaming of getting this one-seater electric car out into the world? Processing all that we had seen, I couldn't stop thinking about social chemistry and how important it is to success in business. You never want to bring someone in who's going to upset the applecart. You can build a pretty good company with the right people. But with the wrong people?

I kept thinking about how much I admired Intermeccanica's close family dynamic. I don't think that can be separated from their craft and dedication. There is an integrity there and a desire to make it work beyond any petty arguments or disagreements. I figured with that dynamic in place, you could make any kind of magic happen.

Counting my lucky stars that I had such a great relationship with the Intermeccanica family, I turned to Henry and asked him sincerely, "Do you think we can put a team together in Vancouver to build our own version of the one-seater electric car?"

Henry looked back at me with raised brows. This was a much bigger ask than what I'd initially invited him down to California for. Instead of manufacturing an already designed and tested vehicle, I was asking him to start from the ground up with me. "I certainly think we can try," he responded. "We know enough people." He started to grin a little, and then a little more. "I'm in," he told me.

I gave him a huge smile and extended my hand. "All right," I said. "Let's do it. Let's move forward."

We shook hands and with that, the Solo and Electra Meccanica were off to the races. Henry saw the same potential I did with the single passenger car. While it made perfect sense, the concept was so off the beaten path that no major manufacturer would risk it, at least not back then. The Solo was a niche product, a realm in which others were too scared to play—which meant that it lined up perfectly with Intermeccanica's values and mission.

I officially acquired the company, offering the Reisner family a lot of money to work with me. I wanted to make sure Henry and Paula knew how much I respected what their family had built. Launching Electra Meccanica wasn't just founding a new company—it was acquiring a legacy. In order to make the deal, I asked Henry what he thought his company was worth, and he said, "Well, what would you pay for it?"

And I said, "I think it's worth $2.5 million."

Henry's brother Edward was sitting there, and he did a spit take because he figured I'd offer $300,000 or something. Then I said I'd give them five million shares of the company, and he did a double spit take. I know he was the one who really spoke to the family afterward. Edward, with his financial business background, was the secret sauce in the deal. As the family was discussing my offer, Edward insisted that if I was offering that much money *alongside* the promise that they could take ownership back if the company didn't work, why wouldn't they take the offer?

Later, people would ask me, "Why did you spend so much? Their market value wasn't even half what you paid them." But you don't lowball these things, right? It was of the utmost importance to me that they knew how much I valued their legacy and what they'd painstakingly taken decades to build.

Even more important than the dollar amount on paper, I wanted to secure Paula's genuine approval. As the matriarch of Intermeccanica, she had final say, and I wanted her to be thrilled at the opportunity for us to come together. When I asked her for her blessing, Paula said yes, but only if I adhered to specific conditions. She asked me to promise her that the "cars will always look good" and to "never let an accountant or a lawyer design the car." I laughed and gave her my word. Now that was a promise I could stick to.

We had an incredible core team of people on board to build the Solo, including general manager Ed Theobold, project manager Bree Sharratt, chassis and finite element analysist Rich Hoyle, mechanical engineer Tammy Yu, and long-time Intermeccanica technician Kevin Relkoff. One of the first calls Henry made was to a Detroit-based designer and old Intermeccanica friend, Rod Trenne. Up for the challenge, Trenne took the job and led the charge on the Solo's unique shape and design, with additional support from designer and model builder Rob King.

To begin production, we shipped in some of the original Corbin Sparrows from the East Coast, and I bought all the stuff a guy named Dana Myers had sitting in a garage in Ohio from the Corbin bankruptcy receiver. Henry used all these odds and ends to hammer together the first four or five prototypes. They were essentially Electra Meccanica Sparrows. They looked ridiculous. But we were able to use them as a development platform to test out the systems we needed for the Solo.

The first thing we did after ripping them apart was change their lead acid batteries and motors to what the motor should be in a Solo. Meanwhile, as Henry was tinkering away, I worked with the engineers and the designers on the ideal layout for a one-person vehicle, which was going to be markedly different than the Sparrow.

Most of the parts we brought in were local. We got the bodies made in New Westminster, the chassis made in Victoria, and other odds and ends from Surrey. While the battery cells came from Korea, we put everything together in Vancouver. The original Solo is a British Columbia–built vehicle through and through.

Originally, the Solo only had one door, which was a total night-mare. I told the team we needed to completely re-engineer the whole thing. That's when Rod Trenne really came into the picture and upgraded the dynamic, including the idea to use aerospace material for the chassis. Rod had experience working on Corvettes and had previously worked with Intermeccanica on developing something like an upscale Corvette before, which Intermeccanica didn't proceed with because it was too expensive. The Solo became their Corvette moment.

The Solo actually has the same seating position as a Corvette. I know that when some people look at the size and shape of the Solo, they go, "Well, I'm a big guy. I can't fit into that thing." That's when I love to drop in the information that the Solo's seat is exactly the same as a Corvette. That catches people's attention and shows them that looking at the Solo from the outside doesn't even come close to telling you everything you need to know about it. Really, you have to experience it.

While we all mourned the fact that we couldn't ask Frank for his input, Paula guided us and gave us priceless ideas and feedback along the way. I tell you, she's still an automotive visionary to this day. No surprise, of course—she comes from sixty years of this stuff.

As we were designing the Solo, we had all these guys sitting around the table, discussing the body and the layout and everything, and Paula comes and looks over our shoulders. She looks at us for a while and then all of a sudden, in her delightful Hungarian-Italian accent, she goes, "Boys, how does a young lady in a skirt get in and out of your car?" We all look at each other and go, "Wow, you're right. You can't get into this thing with anything other than pants." We changed the whole layout for that.

All along the way, I kept coming back to our mission—keep it light and small, build it well, but keep it affordable. Meanwhile, Paula would give notes on the design, making suggestions like tucking it in at the back and making it narrower. She and I both share an appreciation for sleekness. The Solo had to be appealing to the eye and not look like, in Paula's words, "an overweight old lady."

Designing the Solo on the computer was brand new to Paula. She came from the age of pencil and paper, and I could see that she was tentative about this mode of production. But she never said anything against it. I would just see her watching us, thinking, *Let's see what these guys can do.* I knew she was cautiously optimistic, with the key word being "cautiously," as she watched us build the cars in a manner completely new to her.

Fitting the windshield is one of the trickiest parts of building a car, getting it just right. When the windshield arrived, I could read the skepticism on Paula's face. I have pictures of her looking over the buck, analyzing the curves of where the windshield would go. (The "buck" is the solid wood mold of the car with all the grooves and dips and edges carved out, based on a design made on the computer. The prototype windshield gets placed on the buck and is also made from specifics drawn out on the computer.) When Henry picked up the windshield and walked over to the wooden model, Paula was just sitting there, watching and not saying a word. As Henry placed the windshield on the buck, it dropped in perfectly with a satisfying click. You and I know that's what a computer does—it lines everything up perfectly—but for someone with a lifetime of experience in pen and paper? I watched Paula nod, wordlessly, and then carry on with her day ... though I'm pretty sure I detected a slight smile on her face.

A few weeks later, she said to me, "You know, I was really doubtful about this computer technology. I had no idea what this kind of engineering could do. But when I saw Henry put that windscreen in there and it just clicked in perfectly, that's when I knew you were on to something." Pretty special to watch a legend watch her legacy grow into something new, don't you think?

The process of building the Solo took a lot longer than I wanted to, which required a lot of patience. Henry wasn't delivering as fast as he promised he would. I consider Henry a brother as I much as I consider him a friend, but we sure had our challenges.

After we'd finished the design and smoothed out all the kinks, Henry had promised me ten cars a month to start and fifty cars a month thereafter, but at this point he wasn't even producing two cars a month. As with anything, sometimes things are promised to you that take months longer to get done. I did my best to incentivize faster production—if they asked for $30,000, I would give them $50,000 so they'd have extra money for any other parts—but things still wouldn't get done on time.

That's where you have the choice of blowing everything up or shutting your mouth and practicing patience. You have to trust that your people will get their stuff together and figure it out. The key here is to not give up. I mean, really, what are you going to do—go back to driving gas cars? Absolutely not. Because that's the end of the world, right? So, you work your way through things. You never fail until you quit. That's a lesson for any aspiring entrepreneur to remember. And patience. Patience is key.

As the Solo was nearing completion and we were gearing up to take the company public, a very interesting opportunity came along. Well, two interesting opportunities—but we'll get to my political run in the next chapter. When my PR person told me that the next season of *Dragon's Den* (known in America as *Shark Tank*)—a reality TV series where entrepreneurs pitch their business ideas to a panel of venture capitalists in the hopes of securing financial investments from them—was casting, that she'd already contacted the producers, and they were interested in talking to me, I figured why the heck not.

It was a wacky time. I was in the middle of taking Electra Meccanica public *and* running a political campaign. I had never been more stretched or stressed, but I couldn't say no to any of the priceless opportunities that were coming along.

The *Dragon's Den* producers were scheduled to do an evaluation at a hotel in Vancouver not far from our offices, so it was easy to pop over and take fifteen minutes to talk to them about the opportunity. I drove over in my Solo, obviously, and went into the hotel, where there were about two hundred people waiting on chairs in a big ballroom. They had three desks up front where the producers were sitting, and groups would go up one by one to discuss their pitches. When I got up to the desk and began describing Electra Meccanica and the Solo to them, they went, "Really?! An electric car—you're serious? When could we see one?"

I gave them a huge smile and said, "I've got one downstairs."

"Shut up," they responded. "Downstairs?" Then the producers left all two hundred people sitting there as I led them downstairs to look at the Solo, which I'd valet parked. Worth the twenty bucks, right? The producers were thrilled by it, of course, and invited me to come on the show and pitch.

That's how I ended up in Toronto, one month before the election, pitching the Solo on reality TV. I sent the car to Toronto in advance and flew out with our PR person to film the episode. It took about four days out of my already silly-packed schedule, but it was an opportunity I couldn't pass up. Might as well have a little fun while you're shutting down the last gas station, right?

Going on the show wasn't about getting money; it was about getting more publicity. Besides, they said right off the bat that they "don't hand out money." Maybe if you're starting a cafe or a small product line, they would give you some money, but my ask for $25 million? It was outrageous. That's not really what they do there. The producers loved it, of course. It was the biggest ask in the history of the show. They specifically directed me to go in there and be larger than life. "The bigger the better," they said. Naturally, I was happy to oblige.

It's a funny episode to watch now because nobody at that time really got what we were doing, which I love. I come across as pretty mean, actually—and I guess I kind of was because I didn't entertain any of the questions that I thought were silly or stupid. I knew my product and I suspected that they wouldn't understand it.

I went through the whole process thinking about what it would look like watching it back in twenty years. I knew time would be on my side so I didn't suffer any fools. Some of the stuff they edited out was pure gold, but they left a lot of juicy tidbits in there. It was a ton of fun, and I'd do it again in a heartbeat.

After the drama of reality TV and the election campaign, my sole focus was on taking the company public. At a certain point, I realized that if this company was going to be worth $10 or $20 billion, we couldn't have a guy like me with a background in greenhouses running it. We needed an automotive industry expert and the board of directors agreed. That's when I bumped into Paul Rivera and brought him in as CEO. My MO for running a company is to continue surrounding myself with people who are smarter than me until I'm the dumbest person in the room and then leave.

By 2018 we were finally ready to go public, which despite my desire to have things move faster, was shockingly quick. Especially considering the fact that we weren't just taking a three-year-old company public—we were taking a sixty-one-year-old company public. I knew that would play well in the stock market, and it did. The mechanics of taking a company public are pretty brutal but going public is of vital importance if you care about the longevity of your company. Elon Musk taking Tesla public allowed him to continue innovating. If you stay private, only working with investment bankers—who historically are not big dreamers or futurists as they only care about their return on investment—you're not going to have the same experience. Staying private is what Henrik Fisker of the Fisker Karma did, and the company died because of it. When you go public with a great product, as long as you capture the imagination of the general public, they will keep buying your stock, investing in the vision as it were, and forcing the investment community at large to smell the coffee and continue financing your product.

By the time we got to take the whole team to NASDAQ in New York and ring the bell, I was ready to celebrate. This was a Vancouver company going public, a sixty-one-year-old company going public, a family legacy going public on NASDAQ, and everyone there with me was a personal, close friend. It was a truly special day. We'd spent the past three years working together to make this possible. Every single person on that stage had invested between $10,000 and $2 million in helping take the company public—not because they wanted money, but because they wanted to make sure that their kids would have a planet to live on. As we stood there together, cheering, with all the investment people looking up at us, it was dramatic and emotional.

When the company went public, I remember Henry thanking me because I'd completely changed the fortunes of his family. They were a struggling family business. They were in debt. They were making nice cars, but they couldn't get over the hump. And now they're rich. They have large amounts of stock. They renovated their house. Their kids are rich. They could have said no to me, but they decided to make the leap, take the risk. I kept turning it back on them. I said, "You guys were just smart enough to say yes." I admired their legacy deeply, so for them to allow me in was a real honour. I don't know if I would have been able to pull the Solo off with anyone else.

Since its public launch, Electra Meccanica has gone as high as a billion dollars in market cap. So, to the people who questioned me for buying the company for $2.5 million, I'd say that's a pretty shrewd investment. There's no sense in being stingy when you truly believe in your product. I spent a small fortune bringing it to life, and I turned—and squeezed—every stone along the way. After a lifetime of dreaming, my electric car company was officially a reality.

Now there are one-seater cars in development everywhere. Even Frank Stronach, founder of international automotive parts company Magna International, one of Canada's biggest companies, has seen the writing on the wall and is getting into the one-seater game. I've always said, if I'm the only person working on a concept or building a unique company, I've failed. But if it's the first of many, that's what I consider a true badge of success.

With Oma Rosa, Cora, and Irene at the family greenhouse in Port Coquitlam

Outside the Marine Building in Vancouver, 1960s

Traveling with Zuka to California

The day before running the 2013 Boston Marathon

Test mule for the Solo in Vancouver

Early drive system for the Solo

The Sparrow and the Solo

Diesel campaign bus for the BC Greens

Election brainstorming with campaign manager Brittany Whitmore

Onstage at Dragon's Den

Mom and Dad with their "favourite child"

With Bill Nye and the Solo in Los Angeles

Listing Electra Meccanica on the NASDAQ Stock Exchange

At Formula E in Spain with Nick Heidfeld

With Dan O'Day and Ryan O'Connor at the 108th RSNA Scientific Assembly

The first 500 Solos in Mesa, Arizona

THE ELECTION

*The world will not be destroyed by those
who do evil, but by those who watch
without doing anything.*

Albert Einstein

I wanted a plane. A green plane—completely fuelled by a sustainable fuel like algae—to tour across the province and make everyone see that the BC Greens had officially arrived. But the party said no.

When BC Green Party leader Andrew Weaver asked me to run for MLA (Member of the Legislative Assembly) in the upcoming provincial election, he caught me off guard. I was in the middle of taking Electra Meccanica public and busier than I'd ever been. I considered it a huge honour to even be asked, but could I really run?

My home province, British Columbia, had been under Liberal rule for the past fifteen years and our then-Premier, Christy Clark, was set on building a pipeline through the province—using my tax money, no less—to carry oil from Alberta to the Pacific Coast in order to be shipped overseas. Fortunately, I was far from the only one against the pipeline plan and there was a real sense going around that our province wanted something different.

The BC NDP (British Columbia New Democratic Party) had been the official opposition for the last twelve years, and they were leaning in hard to take over. (The Conservative party doesn't have much of a presence in BC. They're only slightly more prominent than, say, the Christian Heritage Party or the Libertarians. If you're unfamiliar with the dynamics of BC politics at that time, think of the BC Liberals as Republican-lites, the BC NDP as union-forward and toe-the-line Democrats, and the BC Greens as the young, scrappy unknowns—climate-forward but quickly growing into something new and different.)

The BC Greens had only ever elected one MLA (Andrew Weaver in the last election) to the Legislature. Despite many British Columbians' interest in the BC Greens, many people felt their only choice to oust the Liberals was to vote for the NDP—a narrative the NDP took in stride, seeding the narrative that if they chose Green, they might "split" the vote and we'd end up with the Liberals again. We had an uphill battle ahead of us.

Fortunately, I love a challenge. I agreed to Andrew's offer to run and I readied myself to climb that mountain without fear. My goals were clear: get Christy Clark out, showcase Andrew Weaver as the brilliant alternative, and win my home riding, Mount Pleasant—a constituency the NDP had owned since the borders of that riding had been drawn.

I knew we had to go big to make a difference, so I told Andrew and his team that I would rent them a campaign bus and we would emblazon his face across the side for all the world to see. The BC Greens had never had a campaign motor coach before and they were thrilled, but the idea of a plane freaked them out. "People will be confused," they said. Or even "upset." That's not the Green Party the public knows and loves. Apparently, it would have been too much of a shock to the people's system.

"Okay, fine," I replied. "We'll just start with the bus."

Which was ultimately fair. It would have been a shock to my bank account too. After all was said and done, I ended up investing six figures into the election. I do sometimes wonder how things would have gone if they'd let me have the plane. Some of the political players got upset when I arrived and started putting real money into the Green Party. They surely would have lost their minds if we'd been flying around.

In truth, a sustainably fuelled plane actually wouldn't have been realistic, as much of a splash as it would have made in the papers. I had my eye on a beautiful jet aircraft from Honda, one with the engines on top of the wings. At the time I was working with Honda on an algae-based biofuel. Unfortunately, this type of plane is not practical yet for short-range trips, which is what is needed for campaigning around BC. (Electric sea planes are, however, practical *and* currently operating in Vancouver for short-range trips through a company called Harbour Air.)

For sustainable fuel, algae are an exciting fuel feedstock that are very easy to produce. All you have to do is make big, sloppy pools full of algae, collect it up, squeeze out the excess water, and process it into kerosene before you throw it into your jet—though the jet must be retrofitted with a fuel tank and fuel lines that accept organic matter, otherwise they will deteriorate. Algae is just one type of SAF (sustainable aviation fuel). There are others that don't require retrofits, and the SAF industry is growing quickly. Dozens of airlines around the world are using SAFs in their planes already (usually a 30–40% SAF blend with fossil fuel), with more converting to SAFs all the time.

Generally, SAFs are biofuels made from waste and excess raw material. Airports (and shipping ports and train stations) are the perfect place to implement this technology because they are massive hubs. Distribution to smaller fuel centres like gas stations is less realistic with biofuel. You're never going to see a biodiesel pump (or hydrogen pump, for that matter) in the middle of Vancouver, unlike electric charging stations, which are (or can be) everywhere.

For our campaign bus, we used biodiesel sourced from a depot in Esquimalt (a town on Vancouver Island). While biodiesel still creates greenhouse gas emissions (keep in mind there are also emissions coming off you and me), biodiesel is *way* less harsh on the environment than fossil fuels because of the reduced emissions and because you don't have to frack it out of the ground. Biodiesel is sourced from waste, like old cooking oil.

While we didn't have a plane, the bus surprised people plenty. As I said, the BC Green Party had never had a campaign bus before. It made a huge difference. It brought us to the next level. Now we were considered one of the big three parties. The bus announced that we'd arrived—and it confounded the media.

I just knew someone was going taunt us with, "How can you call yourselves the Green Party when you're driving around burning fossil fuels?" As if all the other parties didn't have environmental platform promises and weren't burning gas. I coached Andrew Weaver to be ready for that moment. "They're going to come for you," I warned him. "Don't brag about the biodiesel fuel or anything. Just wait for them to dig themselves into a hole."

So, when a reporter raised their hand at one of the first big press conferences and asked, "What's the Green Party doing driving around in a bus? Shouldn't you be on bikes? What about the carbon emissions?" I was watching from the audience with the biggest grin.

Andrew smiled and very calmly and politely laid out all the details of the sustainability of the bus, where it was fuelled up, the emission difference, and so on. Then he asked, "Do the other parties use biodiesel for their transportation?"

Can you imagine what the reaction would have been if we were flying around in a private jet? "How hypocritical are the Greens, not walking the walk." Come on. That's not what we're here to do.

The bus cost about $65,000 to make happen, and it was worth every single penny. In motorsports, if you hire me to represent you as a driver, that's what I'm going to do for you. I'm going to make a big splash so that everybody knows exactly who you are. This is part of how you win. It's not just the talent or who's best for the job—it's also your appearance to the public. When I showed up with my team on day one of an IndyCar race, we did not show up with some paltry little rental car. No way. We would show up with a hospitality booth and a motor coach and five or six of the driver's previous cars, including go-karts, so that people could see their full trajectory. By the time our team hit the track, everyone was cheering for our guys because they'd experienced their history and knew their story. I applied that same mentality to the Green Party. For better or worse, people believe in you more if you show up with an entourage, with toys and flashy things. All of that comes into play in politics.

I'd been supporting the BC Greens for several years before I stepped up to the plate myself. Jane Sterk was the leader when I first started supporting the BC Green Party. I called up their head office sometime in 2012 to see what kind of help they needed. None of the other parties were making any sense on climate or fossil fuels, and I figured they could use my support. The writing was on the wall, and it was pretty upsetting to see the public's general lack of interest in the only party in BC provincial politics who appeared to be aware of the stakes. At the time I got involved, Jane was lobbying Andrew to become the leader of the party, which took *a lot* of convincing on her part. She had to ask him over and over again before he finally agreed.

Andrew holds a master's from Cambridge and a PhD from the University of British Columbia in applied mathematics. He won a Nobel Peace Prize for his work with Al Gore on the UN Intergovernmental Panel on Climate Change and was, at the time Jane asked him to run, teaching climate science at the University of Victoria. Apparently, he was lecturing his students that if they didn't like the way things were run in the world, then they should try to change them—but would then turn around and complain about the state of provincial politics. His students eventually called him out, saying, "Why don't you do something instead of just telling us to do it?"

Andrew Weaver took the position of deputy leader in 2012, the year before his historic win as the first seat for the BC Green Party in the Legislature. Jane introduced us in the lead-up to that election. I'd rented a campaign office on Broadway in Vancouver for all the local candidates, and when I met Andrew, we clicked immediately. He was so sharp, intelligent, and warm—like the Barack Obama of Canadian politics.

After he won that first election, he stepped back from leadership to focus on his job as MLA for the Oak Bay-Gordon Head riding, but once the 2017 election rolled around, Andrew was back as leader again, and in the interim years we'd grown quite close. I'd invite him to speak at the Vancouver Electric Vehicle Association, where I was an active member, to inspire my fellow members to get more involved in politics. Andrew would come in and give rousing speeches, and one night in 2016, as he was prepping to give another talk, we were chatting about the upcoming election.

That's when he extended the offer. He was expressing to me that they needed more good candidates and I responded, half-kidding, "Could you ask these people to run?"

He replied immediately, "I should ask you to run."

As you know, I was about to take my company public and I'd never seen myself as a politician, but as his words started to sink in, the more I thought about it, the more it made sense. As I weighed the scenario in my mind, I asked myself, *What would Howard Hughes do? What would my heroes do?* And I realized they'd do exactly this … Howard would say, "Let's get after it. Let's get it done." It wouldn't matter how busy he was.

Looking at the state of things, how could I not step up and do something? Canada had been spending more money on the oil and gas industry per capita than any other country in the world— despite experts making it crystal clear that it wouldn't be safe for us to burn these fossil fuels *and* how the amount that had already been pulled out of the ground would exceed our emissions targets and destabilize the climate beyond the point of no return. Still our governments continued building and subsidizing fossil fuel projects, not even taking into consideration how every dollar spent on oil, gas, and other nineteenth- and twentieth-century forms of energy is a dollar not spent on innovation and clean technology.

So, to the horror of many people in my life, I decided to take on the challenge of running for office. Neck-deep in taking Electra Meccanica public, my colleagues asked me how I was going to do it all—and stay healthy. Meanwhile, my investment friends clutched their pearls, saying, "Jerry, what if you win? You'll have to move to Victoria. You've got a billion-dollar company to run!" I told them I'd worry about that when it happened. Once I decide to go for something, I put all my weight behind it. No matter the risk.

By December 31, 2016, I'd rented out a space in the Kingsgate Mall—a kitschy and beloved community mall just off Main and Broadway in East Vancouver, smack dab in the centre of the Mount Pleasant riding—*my* riding. As we turned on the lights, I said to my team, "These lights get turned off when the current government is removed." Then I set off to do everything in my power to make a difference—for the future and the current state of the province. And, let me tell you, there was a lot of work to do.

My riding, Mount Pleasant, is one of, if not the most, impoverished ridings in Canada. It is the riding that includes Vancouver's Downtown Eastside. When I went head-to-head with NDP incumbent Melanie Mark, I asked her why she was running for a party that had overseen the riding for three decades but provided no lasting solutions. She didn't answer me. I know she wanted to make a difference, but why choose a party where you're forced to toe the line?

I asked the Liberal candidate Conny Lin those questions too. I said to her, "You seem like a smart person. You've got a solid background. So, what on Earth are you doing running behind somebody like Christy Clark?" I question someone's judgment for doing that. It doesn't make sense. Conny was a good sport about it—we'd go out for drinks once in a while and have wonderful debates.

I met so many wonderful people during that adventure. We opened our space in the Kingsgate Mall for all the Green candidates to use. It was the Vancouver campaign office and the unofficial BC Green Party headquarters. I wanted to make all the Green candidates' campaigns as successful as possible, not just mine. I told my staff explicitly, "Anything the other candidates need, we'll support them. Give it to them, get it done. If they need a desk to work at or want to host an event or need fundraising support, put a volunteer on it and make it happen."

The other candidates were thrilled to have a place to print flyers, take meetings, and just hang out. The Green Party had been operating on a shoestring budget for too long. We developed a real community during that time, but while this was the most access and resources the BC Green Party had ever had, we were still a small-scale operation. Volunteers would go into the back room to take a break and almost trip over Andrew Weaver napping on the floor.

Andrew was great with taking time to talk to people and explain the policies. We even put our most prominent policy points up on the wall, with explanations as to the science behind them. Having this space brought everyone together and united us around the larger cause. That space in the Kingsgate Mall became a hub for the Greens' community building—and, unfortunately, a hub for the NDP's hatred.

The NDP were not okay with our loud and unapologetic presence. They had never seen so many Green signs in their prized riding. We put them up everywhere and they pushed back hard. Melanie Mark's team would come around and speak to the management about how many signs we had—they even picketed with a bunch of volunteers, marching outside, around, and through the mall. People who had agreed to put up signs later asked us to take them down because they were receiving such negative feedback. It was to the point where people were coming up and yelling at them for splitting the vote away from the NDP, which was absurd considering that in the last election (a by-election the previous year), the Liberals had come in third. There were zero real vote split concerns in that riding.

While we did end up with thousands of dollars of fines for putting signs in the "wrong" places, like telephone poles or street planters (the volunteers were later given better training), we adhered to the rules as best we could and made sure we had permission in writing to put up signs on Kingsgate Mall property. When we found out that we were only allowed to have two signs up on the mall property, we ordered two five-by-twelve signs. That didn't go over well with the NDP. As our volunteers were putting the signs up, mall security guards were literally trying to take their tools away, even though we were well within our right to hang those signs.

The signs were just one part of our campaign blitz plan. I knew we had to be big if we were going to have any chance at winning, and I knew we needed to get people pumped up. I'd hired multiple campaign managers to help guide the ship, including a young specialist in marketing and PR. Both of us knew how to engage people's interest and get them pumped up—it's what we do professionally—but there were so many barriers to getting the message out. The rules are strict in the game of politics. We couldn't send out a press release to the paper for them to just publish the information because they had to regulate how much they wrote about each party. It was very different from car racing, and I recognized it as a dynamic challenge. We learned as we went, translating our skillsets into this new world with its bizarre set of rules.

Regardless of the challenges, we did all sorts of fun things to promote the Greens. I had green shirts made up for my running group with the slogan, "It's Time," and we would wear them jogging around town. We'd host events at the Solo showroom, with Andrew giving a speech and answering questions. I threw all sorts of ideas at my marketing team. I suggested a flash mob of volunteers at every gas station in town. I wanted as much press as we could garner.

It was exhausting, but I didn't let my energy fade. The trick when leading a team is to always stay positive and upbeat. You must lead by example. Even when you're worn out and tired, you'd better believe the team is worn out and tired too. It's of no use for your team to see their leader as anything but energetic and motivated. We were there to move the dial forward and make a difference, not complain or fixate on problems.

The Green Party had never experienced a politician quite like me before. My energy level is next level compared to most people. Because I was running on pure passion and not any sort of desire to be a career politician, I had nothing to lose. I wanted to win, sure, and I believed I could win—but it wasn't *about* winning. People could tell that our main goal was to build community, connections, and excitement toward a Green paradigm shift. We received so much positive feedback, especially because people were excited to see the party finally being taken seriously. The Greens weren't fringe anymore. When people saw that we had an office and a bus, they felt confident that they could vote for us now.

The feedback wasn't all sunshine and rainbows. During the campaign, people would troll our accounts on Facebook and Twitter with all sorts of weird stuff. Being the person that I am, I would send them the cheekiest responses—responses it's best not to print here. I would rip people apart instead of candy-coating it. That did not go over well.

Before long, my team took away my social media privileges. A week after they booted me offline, my sister reached out to ask if I was still responding to the comments. She'd read a reply that was something like, "Thank you very much for your input. Although I can understand where you're coming from, here's the other side of the story that we have to address as well." It was very diplomatic. More diplomatic than anything I've ever written. She read it and said, "That's not you, is it?"

In hindsight, I do look at the balanced and measured responses from my team and go, "Huh. You know what? That's not a bad way to put it." I like to be fiery and activating, but there's always a place for calm, measured discussion. Especially in politics.

The crazy thing was, though, that many of the negative social media comments were from people on the NDP's payroll—trolls paid by the NDP to comment divisive things about us! One of my team members noticed a pattern and started to do some digging. What they discovered was that there were about sixteen or eighteen of the same accounts posting the same troll-like comments, and they managed to trace the profiles, including one individual posting under nine different names, back to the NDP. Like clockwork, when any article or post came out, they would immediately interact with it negatively with the primary narrative being that a vote for the Greens was as good as a vote for the Liberals. The NDP was seeding the vote-split narrative.

Once we figured out what was happening, we wanted to stop it, but we didn't have any hard evidence. We realized it would be difficult to prove what we knew without more proof, so we decided to lay a trap. The team wrote up a press release that we knew the media would cover and sent it out. As media outlets ran the article, we prepped about a dozen of our volunteers to get ready to engage with the trolls. When we posted the article to our socials, we targeted it specifically to NDP supporters and followers.

The trap worked perfectly. It was like poking a swarm of bees. Over the course of an hour-and-a-half, hundreds of comments appeared across all threads. Once we knew we'd caught them, we posted a graphic with two troll dolls—one troll had green hair and a big smile, and the other troll had orange hair (the NDP's colour) and a super angry face. "Gotcha," it said. Then we gathered up their handles and made a list of the active, intentional trolls.

After we'd caught them in the act, one of my team members called up a highly-placed NDP politician with whom they had a standing relationship and told them what we'd discovered. My team member told them, "I trust you're not aware of this, but this is what's happening. I'm happy to send you evidence, but I will be sending it to your NDP email address. And this is completely not allowed." Within an hour, all the profiles had either been deleted or we never heard from them again.

The vote-split narrative, at least in Mount Pleasant, was never public opinion. It was seeded by a handful of people employed by the BC NDP. In a weird way, though, it was a bit of an honour as well. No one would have bothered us if they didn't think we were making an impact. I know it wasn't just our large and ever-present signage that triggered them; we were doing some work behind the scenes that also ruffled feathers.

As I explained earlier, the Mount Pleasant riding is home to some of the most devastating poverty in Canada. We spent quite a bit of time walking around the neighbourhood, talking to people and hearing their stories. I never publicized my time down there or used it as a campaign tactic. We didn't go to campaign. I just wanted to know what their reality was like and what we could do to help. We did a food drive and some other things, but the biggest thing they told me they needed was toilets. So, I got them toilets.

As we were arranging the facilities, whether it was for the optics of the election or just the usual police sweeps, the cops were displacing Downtown Eastside residents on the grounds of "unsanitary conditions."

Now, if you think of this as a good thing, you must understand that these folks have nowhere else to go. Their alternatives are government regulated SROs (single room occupancies) or camping out elsewhere in the neighbourhood. These residents made it clear to me that sleeping outside is safer than SROs—which are often mold-infested housing projects where they are at risk of being robbed or harmed by unwell individuals. They are at risk of that on the streets too, but they stxated that they feel safer outside where they are all looking out for each other.

As the police were attempting to evict these people, displacing them for the sake of displacement—an utterly pointless cycle of action that solves zero problems—we requested a permit for the toilets through one of my companies. Being the known business-man that I am, we got instantly approved. The porta-potties were contracted and installed, and wouldn't you know it, when the police showed up, they no longer had the legal right to evict them. Naturally, the property development people or the cops or the NDP or whoever it was that had such a problem with us and our desire to ameliorate people's lives, the city, and our country at large tried to get our permits revoked. Fortunately, in Canada, a contract is a contract, so the porta-potties, and the community, stayed.

Throughout the election, we kept our heads held high and had our fun. I would load up the biodiesel campaign bus with our volunteers and cart them over to Cafe Calabria, my favourite ice cream shop on Commercial Drive, conveniently located right next to Melanie Mark's office. We'd plug the meter full of quarters and enjoy our ice cream out on the sidewalk next to Andrew Weaver's face on the bus, staring out across the street, beyond the passing cars, into the eyes of fuming NDPers. They came out right away telling us we couldn't park there, which was absurd. We paid the meters. I would have been happy to buy them all ice cream cones. That would have been a lot more fun, but I guess being nice and coming over for a friendly hello never occurred to them.

I spent everything I had on that campaign—even the money reserved for food. A year later, the *Vancouver Sun* came out with a story about the election contributions, including a graph of the ten biggest contributors to the election. Numbers one, two, and three were unions, and number four was little old Jerry Kroll. Beneath me was the Aqualini family, the people who own the Vancouver Canucks and my favourite pastry joint, Thierry Chocolates. The graph went orange, red (Liberals), orange, green, and then a red-orange split. The Aqualinis played both sides of the fence, splitting their contributions fifty-fifty between the NDP and Liberals.

I got so many phone calls from the reporter leading up to that article, asking me what the hell I was doing. *What am I doing?* Isn't it obvious? I'm bending the arc of history. (The election contribution rules have since been changed with contribution allowances capped at a much, much lower amount.)

I didn't just bend the curve of politics in Canada or North America. I also bent my own personal curve of what I was capable of, as well as who I knew and who I was connected to, which is, sincerely, my most important asset. It was a real moment in time, one that will never happen again. The undertaking of running for government was an incredible effort and expense, but the whole thing was worth it. I met incredible people, flexed my political opinion in public for the first time, and learned so much about myself.

One of the things I learned is that I'm not as wrong as I think I am sometimes. While we came in second place in the election, 4,500 people in Mount Pleasant agreed with me that Green is the way to go, which was more people than voted for the Liberals, the party coming out of power. Splitting the vote my foot.

It's true that I was incredibly disappointed that we didn't win my riding. I really thought we were going to take it all the way. But seeing Andrew Weaver and his colleagues Sonia Furstenau and Adam Olsen elected to a minority government where the Greens held the balance of power made me feel like it was all worth it. We didn't win the election, but we accomplished what we set out to accomplish. We got Christy Clark out of power, we got Andrew back in, *and* we got more Greens at the table.

The whole experience revealed a lot to me about human nature. Mount Pleasant has voted for the NDP for three decades in a row. It's clear that it can be very hard to get people to change their ways, and by very hard I mean impossible, right? At some point, you just have to take away people's gas cars or pull the cigarettes out of their mouths. That's part of what I learned during that time.

If we understand this, we shouldn't be surprised when Putin invades Ukraine, or when the Republicans refuse to change gun laws. Barack Obama talked about this with Jerry Seinfeld on *Comedians in Cars Getting Coffee*, how some politicians are just dead in the eyes. You go, "Well, that person's being a human being, stuck in their ways, in some sort of a mental loop." You can't expect them to change of their own volition. You just have to escort them out of political office.

We need a better system, one that protects us from politicians staying in power too long. Our current system only seems to stagnate people and suck the life out of them. We know we have to find better ways to work together. We know that that's the real solution. We're all on the same ship, after all. It's time we realized that.

THE HORSE-AND-CART MEN

*It is difficult to get a man to understand
something, when his salary depends
on his not understanding it.*

Upton Sinclair

When I approached the government in 2019 on behalf of Electra Meccanica for a $50 million investment loan, the officials assigned to our file straight up laughed at me. I wanted to expand production of the Solos on home soil by building a proper manufacturing plant, ideally in the Lower Mainland of British Columbia. It was an incredibly exciting prospect—the opportunity to manufacture hundreds and then thousands of Solos to deliver throughout the Pacific Northwest and beyond. We would provide five hundred clean jobs, strengthen the local economy, build a base for more innovation, and inspire Canadians while we were at it. But the government would not come to the table.

This won't be new information to anyone who's tried to innovate throughout history. Governments don't lead. Governments follow. Consider the last energy transition. It took the automobile industry nearly fifty years to dislodge horses from the road. That's five whole decades of pushback against innovation. It was a messy transition, as you can imagine, and not just from all the horse excrement. Businesses and livelihoods were at stake: people's lives, their families' wellbeing. From farriers to teamsters to buggy whip makers, the horse industry was big business run by powerful men—men who didn't want to change jobs, men who got mayors elected.

There was no question that mechanically-propelled automobiles would dramatically alter society. For thousands of years, the speed and distance at which humans could travel was dictated by the carrying capacity of horses. We could only go so far, so fast, and for so long. Horses had limits and, most disturbingly, they produced sloppy, disease-ridden waste in their wake, making epicentres of transportation also epicentres of disease. Self-propelled automobiles of both electric and internal combustion engines (they were invented around the same time; internal combustion engines won out due to faster advancements in their technology) blew the carrying capacity of horses out of the water. Cars were a complete game changer, a transformative energy shift on par with the discovery of the wheel.

But the horse industry wasn't interested in an energy shift. They didn't see cars as an opportunity or a technology to embrace and champion. They saw cars as competition, as threats coming for their jobs. So, desperate to stay in power, they turned to the government to impede the transition. And the government, always quick to attend to the status quo (or perhaps never separate from it), complied. Instead of following the natural trajectory of the cart-to-car shift and overseeing a robust energy transition, they created policies that stagnated and impeded the evolution of transportation.

The Locomotive or Red Flag Acts, initially introduced in the UK for steam-powered locomotives, were a particularly absurd set of laws that made driving an automobile as inconvenient as possible. Under these laws, automobiles were required to have multiple mechanics on hand at all times (no taking your shiny new wheels out for a solo spin), your speed was restricted to slower than that of a bicycle (you legally couldn't go faster than 2 mph in the city), and—here's the real kicker—it was mandated that every automobile must always be preceded by a man on foot waving a red flag to announce the automobile's arrival. I'm not kidding. Can you even imagine that? A man walking ten feet in front of your car, side stepping horse shit, waving a flag to warn others that your automobile was incoming. Ridiculous.

The horse industry and their pocketed politicians clearly didn't understand the inevitability of automobiles. If they did, they wouldn't have gone against the rising tide, because nobody wants to go down in history as the idiot who obstructed and stagnated innovation because of their own self-interest and ignorance. Right?

We're in the middle of another transformative energy shift, and when it comes to status quo industry and government, things are only marginally better than they were at the turn of the twentieth century. The political will and drive to follow the natural trajectory of innovation is as dubious as ever. Meanwhile, everything else is amplified, especially the stakes. It is difficult to believe that by this point anyone could underestimate the severity of the climate and ecological crisis, but when your government buys a bitumen pipeline the day after declaring a climate emergency, you start to wonder what's going on. Did these politicians really sign off on the latest IPCC report, or did their assistants do it while they were cheers-ing in the back room with oil barons?

Canada's economy was built on natural resources, so a transition was always going to take time, but never has it been so transparently obvious that we need to divest from harmful, extractive methods of making money as quickly as is safe and possible. Because while the climate crisis has worsened to the point that the Earth's ability to sustain human life over the long-term is now a huge question mark, our government's policy decisions continue to demonstrate that either they do not understand the definition of "emergency" or, worse, that they understand the state of emergency but do not have the capacity or the desire to attend to it with the urgency, efficiency, and aptitude the situation demands.

There are many ways to approach the crises at hand, and all of them require innovative thinking. As Albert Einstein once famously explained, "A new type of thinking is essential if mankind is to survive and move to higher levels" (The Real Problem is in the Hearts of Men). For example, instead of chopping down old growth forests, we develop sustainable second growth practices. Instead of giving billions of dollars in subsidies to oil and gas, we fund electric car infrastructure and local electric car production. Our government is stuck in old ways of thinking, doing, and being. When we remember that province after territory after province is full of brilliant minds ready to redefine Canada as a country who exports clean technology, green innovation, paradigm-shifting biotech and medicine, and infinite creative resources like art, music, film, and literature—if only they had the support—then we understand the urgency of funding innovation now.

The Canadian government has a long history of actively inhibiting innovation. Some of you may remember the Avro Arrow, the world's greatest supersonic fighter-bomber aircraft. Developed in the 1950s at aircraft manufacturing company Avro Canada, the Arrow was as spectacular an innovation as Canada had ever seen. It was faster than any jet in its class, travelling nearly twice the speed of sound, and boasted the world's first computerized flight control and weapons system. Praised around the world for its power and beauty, the Arrow outstripped anything anyone had ever done in aircraft technology and helped establish Canada as a world leader in scientific research and development.

But in February 1959, Prime Minister John Diefenbaker cancelled the program. Overnight, ten thousand people lost their jobs, and by July, all the Arrow aircrafts had been dismantled and every blueprint, model, and design destroyed. It was a complete betrayal of Canada's aerospace industry. Many of our best engineers left the country shortly thereafter and went to work for the US space program and other initiatives where they were free, able, and encouraged to innovate. The reason for the Avro Arrow's abrupt and devastating cancellation was never made clear, though rumours swirled that it came down to Diefenbaker's petty distaste for the company's president, Crawford Gordon Jr.

I've dealt first-hand with both the provincial and federal governments' ignorance around innovation. Our $50 million ask for Electra Meccanica was just a starting point. Frankly, we were willing to take whatever they would offer to break ground. This was shortly after we'd gone public, and we were chomping at the bit to scale up production. I did everything in my power to get the pitch just right. I even hired Michele Cadario, one of the Liberals' own, to lobby them. With her experience as chief of staff for Christy Clark and Paul Martin, I figured if anyone could get the Liberal government on board with supporting the production of the Solo, it would be her. We knew our ask was aligned with the Liberals' proposed innovation agenda, but we also knew they'd never seen anything like us before. A Canadian-made, three-wheeled electric car? Yeah, this was the first time they'd heard a pitch like that.

We thought we might have an uphill battle ahead of us, getting the government on board with something so cutting edge, but we figured the timing was right and with a little imagination, they would understand just how revolutionary the Solo could be. And really, one only has to consider how often people drive alone and how much space our cars take up to understand the importance of the Solo. You don't use your laptop when you walk along the sidewalk to check your email; you use a smaller device that's mission specific. Most car trips are taken solo: running errands, visiting friends, driving to and from work. Just look at the carpool lane on the highway; it's never full. So why do we all use big, bulky cars when all we need is to get ourselves, and sometimes a few groceries, from A to B?

North American cities are dominated and shaped by roads and the space required for parking. Cars everywhere, parked or in motion, take up more space than pedestrians, more space than bicycles and strollers; cars take up almost as much space as the places we live and work. Most people are out there driving by themselves, burning fuel and taking up needless space. The Solo—an electric car that takes up only the space it needs and nothing more—isn't just an energy shift. It's a cultural shift. The Solo is a logical solution to many of our transportation problems, and the only reason there is so much resistance to it is because it's a new concept, something we haven't seen before, and that can scare and upset certain types of people—like the number crunchers, for example. For folks on the street, it genuinely brings joy into people's lives. You get more looks in a Solo than you do in a Lamborghini. Kids, adults, people of all ages and backgrounds point, wave, and cheer whenever I drive by. (Test drive one yourself and you'll see what I mean.)

Michele lined up a meeting and we flew out to Ottawa. Walking around Parliament, I knew I'd hired the right individual when every second person looked up in recognition and said hi to her. Excitement I hadn't yet allowed myself to feel bubbled up as we walked into the Head of Finance's office and began our pitch. Our request was for funding to build a manufacturing plant on Canadian soil, ideally in Abbotsford, but we were open to wherever made the most sense. We were willing to compromise and to partner with provinces other than BC. We told them a $50 million investment would be ideal, but that we were willing and thrilled to work with them and whatever support they could provide.

We finished our pitch, and the Head of Finance was enthusiastic. I was actually blown away by his eagerness. Suddenly, it didn't seem like an uphill battle after all. Maybe everything was going to line up. He even waved off our concessions of a $5 or $10 million starting point and told us they wanted to support us with the full $50 million and that he couldn't wait to see our official proposal. I couldn't believe that this was actually going to happen: a home-grown Canadian electric car company—designed, manufactured, and built on Canadian soil with Canadian hands and brains and hearts and with so much potential to grow. We were actually doing it; the tide had turned.

But then … nothing. We submitted the official proposal, bounced back and forth over a few conference calls, and nothing: complete radio silence. We'd hired contractors, spent a ton of money, and put the whole proposal together. We gave them all the data, the projections, and nothing. I became frustrated and dismayed, but we kept following up anyway—and they kept ignoring us. We continued to ask for updates, continued to ask what was going on, continued to ask for support and communication, asking and asking and asking until I realized that we would go out of business if we waited any longer. That's when I understood that they would never actually say no. That they would just delay, delay, delay until we finally went away. So, we decided to move, to carry on without them. I hired a new CEO, we raised a bunch of cash, and we turned to the United States for support.

I still get trashed on internet forums today for "selling out." But the truth is that I did everything in my power to keep my company in Canada. It simply wasn't possible. I like to think that the federal and provincial governments wouldn't be this ignorant today. But because of how they behaved in 2019, the biggest electric car company in Canada moved to Arizona. That's five hundred clean jobs—plus all the ancillary job potential—drained to the United States of America.

It still breaks my heart thinking how cool it would have been to build these cars locally. The brain drain of our best engineers and innovators (and artists and creatives) forced to leave the country for better opportunities is very real. We're educating incredibly brilliant, talented people here in Canada, and after graduating they move down to San Francisco or over to Boston or elsewhere in the United States. There are engineers all across Canada who get trained up in mechatronics and have nowhere to work at home. I know because I've hired them to go work for me in Arizona.

That's why I feel a great responsibility in my work, and why my priority is to keep my business thriving. As an innovator and a businessman, my job is to make the best possible decisions for my company so we can *continue* innovating and developing and building the technologies society needs. Someone's got to do it and in as effective and efficient a manner as possible. We can't afford to wait around. Companies go out of business waiting for bureaucracy to get on board.

While urgency isn't something the governmental bureaucratic system understands, it is something my fellow entrepreneurs know above all else. Like Elon Musk. He's developed and is delivering some of the most affordable clean technology in the world. Tesla is now providing the lowest cost solar panels in America. That easily could have been a government-led initiative. Imagine what kind of innovations we could fund with the $14 billion a year the Canadian government gives in public financial support to oil and gas.

Today, Elon Musk's Tesla is the largest electric car company in the world, and that's thanks in part to the government of California, who championed his work, giving $500 million to Tesla when they needed it most. Now the company is worth hundreds of billions of dollars. And yes, that initial loan has been repaid.

Eventually, the Canadian federal government did get back to us about our investment ask—after the news broke that Electra Meccanica was opening a manufacturing plant on the other side of the border. But by the time they reached out, it was too late. We'd committed to producing Solos in the States. When they reached out over the phone, one of the government guys confessed to my colleague that they were laughing behind our backs the whole time. After one conference call he told him that they hung up and said, "These guys are dreaming with their electric cars. That will never happen in Canada."

That really hurt to hear. Not that we were being made fun of—I stopped caring about that kind of thing a long time ago—but to know that the government could be so ignorant and blind to a lucrative emerging industry that would benefit the planet instead of degrading it. It was beyond frustrating. Because it's not just me and my business affected by their ignorance, but all Canadians. All Canadians suffer when there are no clean jobs, and everyone suffers everywhere when our economy is dependent on exploiting resources in a manner that directly compromises our health and safety.

I asked Michele, our Liberal lobbyist, to explain why she thinks the government didn't step up. She is a bit more generous than I am with what unfolded. According to her, there was a great deal of excitement on the political side, but the political side—the elected officials—don't make the decisions or do the due diligence on the kind of money we were asking for. It's the analysts, the number crunchers behind the scenes, who evaluate these proposals. And these analysts have rules and regulations to follow. Essentially, she says, they have to tick all the right boxes before they can hand any money over. And Electra Meccanica's Solo didn't fit neatly into any of their boxes.

It's not every day that a new car company starts, never mind one in Canada, and even though automobile manufacturers have always been a big provider of jobs, the Solo is different from traditional automobiles. Michele suggests that the Solo befuddled the government. Because the Solo is not just a one-seater electric car but also a technology, Michele says that the government needed more time to be educated and brought on board with the concept because, "Uniqueness is hard for a government to be nimble enough to figure out in any kind of quick fashion. Electra Meccanica is a technology company that happens to be making cars, rather than a car manufacturing company that happens to be electric. It's a different kind of mindset [that the number crunchers] didn't have the infrastructure to be able to truly understand or bring forward in a fast enough timeframe."

The people doing risk analysis couldn't think outside of the box. There was a traditional automotive box and a technology box, and they couldn't comprehend a company that straddled both. And on top of all that, these decisions were being made by people in Ottawa who were used to driving on icy roads in forty-below weather, making it even more difficult for them to see the value of the Solo, a car that thrives on the West Coast.

I agree with Michele that the government needs to commit to a new approach, but personally I think it's a bit of an apologist attitude to blame it on the number crunchers and the boxes we didn't fit into. We know governments have never been the first or the fastest, whether it's because they're in bed with industry or simply because their bureaucratic structure doesn't allow it.

When it comes to innovation in Canada, we have to blame it on a lack of motivation, plain and simple. If Prime Minister Trudeau said, "This is going to happen. Make it happen," do you think some number cruncher would tell him no? Absolutely not! Imagine if Elon Musk called him up and said, "Do you want to have dinner and talk about building a car factory in Canada?" Do you think Trudeau would even blink before saying yes? The only thing he might ask first, eyes wide, would be, "Will there be media?" So, no. There are zero excuses for the government's lack of support in Electra Meccanica.

It wasn't just the federal government that left us hanging. The provincial government didn't step up to bat either. If we'd had the province working with us, it would have reduced the risk for the feds and strengthened our chances at receiving support. If the BC government had rallied behind us, we would already be moving Solos off the production line. But at the time, the BC NDP were not interested in coming to the table whatsoever. Collaboration with the provincial government was a total non-starter. It was worse than the silent treatment we got from the federal government. Ironically, our Electra Meccanica offices are in Minister of the Environment George Heyman's riding. He's never called or come by even once.

The best support the BC NDP government has shown for the electric vehicle sector is a handful of charging stations and some rebates for new vehicle purchases. These are necessary things, sure, but they're not creating jobs; they're not building up industry. And it's not just my company or electric vehicles that are being ignored by the BC NDP—it's all innovation. They're barely coming to the table with real money for anyone. There are governing bodies and institutions that fund grants and opportunities for individuals and businesses to innovate, but the money is peanuts compared to the support the BC government provides to the oil and gas industry.

Meanwhile, when you turn to the States, they're hungry to support innovation. To build our Electra Meccanica manufacturing plant, we experienced a bidding war between Arizona, Tennessee, North Carolina, and Florida. They were literally fighting over us, offering us huge support packages. To this day, my team is still fielding offers, and I have folks calling me up and asking to talk to my people, wanting to know what we can make happen. They're calling me, actively pursuing my business! They *want* to invest and innovate. It's such a different feeling than anything I've experienced in Canada.

I do get calls now from various levels of Canadian government, asking if we can work together. They seem to be reaching out more and more, clearly beginning to understand the importance of what we're doing. But it's nowhere near fast enough.

We are currently in the most precarious of positions. Innovations in biotech and longevity medicine have us prescribed to be alive, mobile, and healthy longer than ever before, but the climate and ecological crisis continues to worsen each day. As the predicted lifespan of humans reaches two hundred years old and beyond, we're facing massive uncertainty about the state of the planet and its ability to sustain human life. Every minute spent clinging to the past costs us dearly. We could be building momentum toward real solutions, changing the very fabric of our society, but instead we're chopping down ancient, irreplaceable forests and doubling down on pipeline production.

We need politicians with vision, politicians who aren't beholden to dying industries. The government must employ new ways to analyze risk, ways that properly account for the variables of how innovation disrupts traditional industries. Companies that are true innovators are always going to have a different risk profile, and we need people who can properly analyze these projects—analysts who understand technology and who can see outside the box and into the future. If the government wants to play any sort of a role in the emerging technology and innovation worlds and not leave everything up to angel investors in the private sector or let all our brainpower drain to the States, then they need to develop adaptable systems to keep up with evolving risk profiles. We have to keep pushing back against archaic values and stagnant systems. We must keep demanding better. We don't have any time to waste.

With Jevitty, we're innovating beyond government stagnancy. As the Solo redefines the way we drive, Jevitty will redefine the way we live. If the Solo represents a ripple shift in transportation culture, Jevitty is a tidal wave. Culturally, to recognize aging as a disease and to implement the biotech necessary to prevent it—and to ensure this technology is made available to *everyone* as quickly as possible—will no doubt require significant government support.

Canada doesn't have to be the country that shovels minerals out of the dirt, extracts oil from the ground, or chops down ancient, irreplaceable trees. We can protect our natural resources. We can build anew. We can be known for our technology and our ingenuity, our art and innovation, our commitment to a healthy planet and healthy people. There are good people everywhere working toward this. I am just one of them.

PEOPLE, PLANET, PROFIT

Doing less harm is no longer enough.

John Elkington

The state of the world always comes down to individual action and responsibility. While there are systemic factors at play keeping us stuck in an age darker than it needs to be, it's human behaviour that shapes and guides those systems—human behaviour that is overwhelmingly shaped and guided by access (or lack thereof) to that thing we all need to survive: money. That means the sad reality is that if something makes someone money, they will defend it. No matter the environmental or human cost.

Once upon a time there was a "magic mineral" known as asbestos. First mined in Quebec in the 1870s, asbestos was considered Canada's gold. A needle-like fibre, asbestos was ubiquitous, used in products as varied as building insulation, children's playdough, coffee pots, and clothing. Today, you may only be familiar with asbestos as a dangerous and toxic substance, but it wasn't until the 1960s that people began to realize that asbestos might not be safe—and it wasn't until the late 1970s that they started to do something about it.

For the small town of Asbestos, Quebec, the site of a massive asbestos mine, the name came with endless baggage. While the mine shut down in 2012, the town, now known as Val-de-Sources, didn't change their name until 2020. Many were reticent to let the name go, despite the issues it gave them (such as when crossing the border), because the mine and the mineral had been a boon for the town, providing thousands of well-paying jobs for decades. Despite all the evidence, including the deaths of their own miners, many wanted to keep the mine open and keep the town identified by its toxic namesake.

A person's livelihood changes their perception of what's right and what's wrong. If your sole source of income is an industry that's damaging to other people, but it's what feeds your family, you're going to be protective of it.

Fortunately, the asbestos industry eventually got shut down—but it was shut down too slowly, too long after the truth came out, and at the expense of too many lives. Because asbestos was killing people, we had to take those jobs away. Just like we took jobs away from the people in the tobacco industry. Just like we're taking jobs away from people in the oil industry. This is necessary progress. You can't hide behind your dinner table and say that the food on the table is the reason why you need to kill the planet or other people.

All these men and women in the oil and gas industry—and I'm talking less about the workers, the drillers, and so forth, and more about the chief financial and executive officers, the ones who get handed the climate change carbon emission reports and the ones who put out press releases that say, "We're producing the cleanest oil in history," are rationalizing their own deaths. They're finding creative ways to lie to themselves so that they can keep destroying the planet. Why? Because they like the money their job provides. Because they're living in a fantasy land where their own comfort and security is more important than the future of the planet.

The gas car is dead, and it didn't happen because a politician said it was the right thing to do or because the gas industry realized that it was causing damage to its home ecosystem. The gas car is being phased out because electric battery technology was developed by people who understood what needed to be done and followed through on it, entirely at their own expense. This is how the initial automobile happened, how the VCR happened, how motorized flight, and how many, many reality-shifting innovations have happened. Innovation happens because bright, individual minds, communities, and organizations take risks and follow through on their missions.

That's why I get frustrated when politicians want to tax innovators more. If the government had a better track record for funding necessary innovation, I'd be singing a different tune. But they don't, so you'll understand why I have zero interest in paying more taxes than I already do. I have a plan for every last dollar in my bank account. I put my own money at risk, and the government wants to take it and build a pipeline? Not on my watch. I can do better with that money than they ever will—at least the way they're currently operating.

Governments are more than capable of innovating technology—just look at the internet. The internet as we know it today would not have existed without generous investments from the United States government. So, it is possible for our political system to pull the future forward. All we need is political will: a commitment to radical and necessary change. There is too much talk about "where will the money come from," not enough dedication, and nowhere near enough imagination. When you're investing in the future, you must trust that the risk will pay off.

I have always been relentlessly dedicated to my companies. There have been many times when I was paying myself absolutely nothing, living off my savings, and edging closer and closer to the red (and sometimes digging into it), all in the name of getting the company off the ground. Meanwhile, every expense that was needed, I would pay for. Nothing spared and no corners cut—launching the product was always the priority.

Up until about three years ago, when I brought in more executives to Electra Meccanica, I wasn't making any money. The executives looked at my lack of paycheque and said to me, "You can't have the CEO making no money. It looks unusual." They insisted that I receive an income, and a high one at that, and started paying me $300,000 a year.

This frustrated me. I wanted the investors to know that I was in it with them. That if the stock didn't perform well, I would be out just like they would be. But the executives are smarter people than me, which is why I brought them in, so I listened. Everything I do is in service of getting the company off the ground as quickly and efficiently as possible.

I know money is difficult to talk about because so many people struggle with it. For the most part, we can't survive without it. That's why I advocate for a universal basic income. The government has to recognize that you can't have people out starving in the streets, that the infrastructure of a society is only as good as the weakest link in the chain. I know that every capitalist understands what that means. A universal basic income would strengthen the economy in the long run.

We have so many things backwards. We're paying police to sweep the streets and "deal" with crime instead of paying to get people into houses and into mental health programs. When we fund policing and punishment-based services, it keeps perpetuating the problem, but if we funded solution-based services, it would solve the problem. By addressing issues at their roots, we create an ecosystem that allows society to grow and flourish. If we don't plant a seed in good soil, it's not going to grow well. Why is this so difficult for governments to figure out?

We can't begin to comprehend all the ways that housing and feeding people will affect society for the better. Maybe the next brilliant, innovative mind that's going to save the planet is down and out on the streets because they were dealt a bad hand in childhood. Getting those people support is just as urgent as closing the last gas station and curing aging. It's all connected. We want to be proactive in every way possible. It's like the shift from sick care to health care. That stuff's just basic. It needs to be done. Why would anyone be okay with a society where people are unhoused and starving?

It really won't be that difficult to implement the necessary changes. Innovators and entrepreneurs pivot every day. We just have to focus on the outcomes and course-correct accordingly. It will mean applying a little bit more logic, a lot more will power, and using the systems we already have to propel us forward.

For example, I know a lot of people like to harp on capitalism, but does it have to be the enemy? What if, with a little more imagination, we could make the tweaks necessary to have capitalism work for everyone? There's an elegance to that system. I love that it's almost like a storybook fantasy where a little kid who has a dream can make that dream come true. They start by selling their lemonade on the side of the road and can build their dream into a multi-national lemonade company. It's a Cinderella story. That kind of stuff doesn't happen in communist regimes, where your government tells you what you can or can't do.

The downside to capitalism is that you have the right to spend your money on anything. It doesn't have to be something that betters you or the planet. You have the right to pour your money into alcohol at the club or to buy cheap, disposable, useless plastic products. You are free to do anything and then free to complain about the repercussions later on. That's where we could use a little more elegance and a little more incentive, right? How do you get people to take care of themselves and take care of the world around them?

Right now, we're dealing with the repercussions of that overconsumption—of burning fossil fuels to produce products that are going to end up in a landfill after one or two uses. Thanks to companies chasing profit margins and fossil fuel industries actively obscuring information and lying about the reality of climate change, we are now teetering closer and closer to societal collapse. And this is not just about the weather getting too hot or too cold— it's about the food chain breaking or large areas of Earth becoming uninhabitable and forcing mass migration, which would lead to climate refugees and scarce resources and more and more compounding problems.

Like pandemics. Pandemics are aggravated by the world getting warmer. We've got problems with bigger bugs too, like Zika mosquitoes coming up north of the equator and all other sorts of invasive species and diseases spreading around the planet. We've got droughts and floods happening, forcing people to flee their homelands, causing chaos at borders, which in turn fosters racism, negative nationalist ideologies, and strain on the existing support systems in the countries they turn to.

It's easy to get lost in frustration or upset, so we have to remember that we have all the solutions. We cannot lose sight of the reality that there are good people out there working on every problem.

Every single one. All we have to do is implement the solutions and become proactive instead of reactive—like creating an economy that's centred around advancing industries instead of dying indus-tries and building a thriving innovation system that fortifies our future instead of compromising it.

We're going to have to leave behind a lot to accomplish this. Like the useless landfill-headed items. Like the industries created just to move stuff around. Sincerely. How many pointless products and industries are out there today? Planned obsolescence is a problem for the consumer, but not for the companies who continue to reap profits from poorly produced products. Shouldn't your product be so well made that people don't ever have to buy a new one? Too many industries don't have an endgame. How many companies and industries are self-perpetuating, putting a Band-Aid on the wound instead of preventing the damage in the first place? We want products that last and problems that end.

I've been a member of the Vancouver Electric Vehicle Association for about thirty-five years, and it's almost redundant at this point. Electric cars are everywhere now; we don't have to advocate for them anymore. We don't have to sit and meet with government people and explain what a plug-in for an electric car is. What a beautiful thing to become obsolete. We fulfilled our purpose. The real mission for many companies and industries should be to eliminate themselves. That's true success.

Think about the untold billions poured into fighting cancer and other diseases. We want those industries to become obsolete too. Can you imagine a world beyond them? A world where the cancer researcher is out of a job because we found a cure?

How, where, and when we work is changing and will continue to change dramatically. As the automation of jobs continues, as technology evolves and industries orient to toward obsolescence, work will become less about necessity and more about passion.

We're transitioning away from the jobs where someone is screwing the cap on a toothpaste tube. That job has been automated, and we're getting to the point where many, many other jobs will become automated too. Not to mention all the jobs AI has its eyes on … from grocery store clerks to long haul truckers to creative industries and beyond, thousands upon hundreds of thousands of jobs will disappear over the coming decades.

And the point is *not* to create new jobs in their place. When one piece of equipment takes up one hundred jobs, you don't invent one hundred new jobs. That's just wasteful and unnecessary. That's why a universal basic income is not a choice. It's going to happen. This is the vision the early twentieth century had for the future: lives of leisure where we're all working less—or working because we *want to*. It's only because of the flaws in the capitalist system that as automation and AI came on board, we continued working harder than ever.

Even for jobs that don't get automated, everything is shifting. The forty-hour, five-day work week is dying. It's been shown again and again that people can be more productive in less time. There have been successful pilot programs demonstrating this all over the world. Even the BC Greens staff have moved to a four-day work week. The forty-hour work week is a holdover from the industrial revolution. The fact that most people are still holding onto it is pure silliness.

If you work for me, I don't care how many hours you work as long as you get the job done. If you come for only thirty minutes a week but you bring in an investor worth $5 million, I will personally drive you to the airport and fly you to Hawaii and tell you to not come back until you're good and ready. Meanwhile, if you're only charging me $1 an hour, but you're not getting anything productive done, I will fire you. It's not about how much time it takes. It's about the results—the results and how efficiently you arrived at them.

A successful business is an industry consolidator, one where you're pulling in different components as you go so you become more and more streamlined. Did you know that Tesla acquired a company that builds factories? It was the company from Germany that Tesla contracted to build their first gigafactory, and then they realized that they might as well buy it since they knew they were going to need more factories, ones specifically tailored to their needs. Now Tesla doesn't just build machines; they build the machine that builds the machines.

That's the sort of expansive thinking that made Elon Musk a billionaire: approaching building his business from all different angles. It's such a simple solution once you arrive at it but getting there takes practice. It only looks easy from the outside. It's easy to get stuck in narrow-minded thinking, especially when you're stressed out. And it's easy to get stressed out when you're dealing with pushback, naysayers, government obstacles, and gatekeepers married to dying industries.

That's why it's good to develop skills and interests outside of your work and business endeavours. Whether that's exploring hobbies, taking on side projects, organizing in your community, or undertaking activist endeavours, you need something to keep you alive and thriving that isn't related to your business goals.

For me, getting my pilot's license helped me develop a deeper perspective on life and business. It expanded my mind but also grounded me in many ways. Training to fly planes gave me a whole new skillset that in turn bolstered my confidence to do other intimidating things, like going into politics. It's amazing the perspective you get from being up in the air, the feeling of possibility and potential that it instills in you. I really feel like I earned it too. Learning how to interact and communicate with people at two hundred miles an hour in a congested airspace without killing yourself or anyone else—that's an impressive thing. And to be the first person in my whole family tree's history to pilot themselves—that's a powerful thing too.

It took a lot of time and effort to get me to the place where I could even get into the pilot's seat—to build up the confidence to apply and then to find the right place to learn. I was looking into schools for ten years before something clicked. I felt some disappointment along the way, but instead of wondering why it wasn't lining up, I just accepted that it wasn't the right time yet.

Having my pilot's license has armed me against doubt, depression, and failure. (And between you and me, I'd take my pilot's license over a college degree any day.) I think accomplishing this kind of thing—whether it's a pilot's licence or a motorcycle license or a scuba license—provides you with extra armour to face the world and all its challenges. It's like adding tree rings to your trunk; you become a stronger individual by overcoming those risks and self-doubts. Moving forward, all other feats become just a little bit easier. Then when you face failure or come up against fear, you know you have resources and are capable of overcoming those challenges.

When you remember that you are the person who became a pilot or the person who ran for government, you give yourself more license to take chances and risks, like starting your own business or trying out new ventures that perhaps you might not have had the confidence for otherwise. Risk-taking builds confidence.

I really encourage you to do this—to face the scary thing head on and realize that you're not going to die. To experience the wonder, awe, and confidence that floods in afterward. It will have you thinking, *What other risks could I take? What else could I achieve?* There's always a broader perspective to take when faced with *any* problem. Every time you take a risk, you widen your perspective and allow yourself to move forward without (or at least with *less*) fear.

I know that I'm able to do what I do, see what I see, and risk what I risk only because my life has been a series of leaning into what I've been afraid of. This kind of behaviour is available to everyone, if only they give themselves permission. I was recently speaking to Cam Brewer, another friend from the BC Green Party, about green banks and densifying neighbourhoods—real solutions to climate problems—and he had this to say about my work ethic:

"Jerry's put his own money at risk. And he is one of those thinkers who has such a lateral kind of view on the world. There's nothing pigeonholed about him in terms of his thinking. It's wide and vast and his ideas are—for my more conservative mind—some of them are just crazy. But there's always this kernel of logic and foresight. It's not crazy; it's daring and risky, and I really value that in him."

While I most certainly appreciate his kind words, I'm not sharing them to boost my ego. I'm sharing them because they perfectly describe the kind of thinking that leads to BHAGs: Big Hairy Audacious Goals. The kind of goals where you're almost too scared to tell people your ideas because they're so big and so audacious and so revolutionary that you know not everyone is going to understand them.

Everybody has a BHAG—even if it's buried down deep, it's in there. That's what I want to inspire you to go after, the, "Wow, what if I could really do that?" goal and mission. That's what the world needs right now and what the world will continue to need more and more of in the future.

The best way to figure out your BHAG is to ask yourself, "What lights me up?" Ask yourself what you would do if you knew you could accomplish anything. Because that's what you should do! That's your BHAG. There's no need to be embarrassed or scared. And there's no need to listen to anyone but yourself. If you know your mission, it's time to see it through. And if you don't already have a BHAG, allow me to offer you an exercise that will help get you there. Because this is exactly what the world needs right now—all of us leaning into our dreams and making our wildest visions a reality.

What's Your Mission-Based Business?

This is the exercise I recommend to people when they come to me asking for advice. A lot of people want to know what kind of business they should do where they're not going to lose money or waste their time. But I can't give the same advice to everyone. What you should do depends on who you are.

Try this if you're looking for your mission-based business, and I bet something wonderful and unexpected will pop into your head. Either way, I promise it's guaranteed to make you smile and give you insights into your purpose.

Start by sitting somewhere quiet, all by yourself. Shut out any noise around you so everything's completely silent. Get quiet and still and take a few deep breaths. Now imagine winning $100 million. Keep your eyes closed and really feel it, the excitement and the joy. Think about all the things you'd do, the houses and the cars and all that. Maybe you go travelling for a couple of years, see the pyramids and the Eiffel Tower. Now imagine yourself coming back to your new home. You've still got $90 million in the bank, and you wake up on a Monday morning. You've got all the money you need to do whatever you want and all the time in the world. Now, what do you do with your day? How do you fill your time now that you have the resources to do *anything*?

This is the thing that you're going to be great at, no matter what, because it's not about the money. You're not doing it because someone forced you to do it or because you feel guilty. You're doing it because it is a part of who you are—it is your mission.

You might have some stuff come up where you go, "Wow, I can't do that. I'm not an astronaut," or whatever. But if you think about it hard enough, take your time, and start looking at it from different angles, often you can figure out how that impulse and that dream can become a real part of your life.

I did this exercise a long time ago and car racing popped into my head. I had no interest in being a car racer, so at first, I didn't know how I could be involved. But then I realized that I had all kinds of enthusiasm for supporting car racers and understood that I could get involved as an agent for sponsorships. That meant I wasn't putting my life at risk, but I still got to work with my passion. This was the realization that got me out of the flower business and propelled me forward. And look at where it led me to.

I wish the same for you.

UNDERSTANDING AGING

There is nothing in biology yet found
that indicates the inevitability of death.
This suggests to me that it is not at all
inevitable and that it is only a matter
of time before biologists discover what
it is that is causing us the trouble.

Richard Feynman

When your physician sends you a book that says, "The first person that will live forever has already been born, and it could be you," you sit up and listen. When scientists and doctors tell you that if you're eating properly, getting enough sleep, not doing drugs or drinking too much alcohol, maintaining a positive outlook on life, exercising often, and not leading a sedentary life that now you have the potential to live forever ... well, that's when you start a company to help get the news out. Longevity is for everyone, and Jevitty is here to help.

We're on a two-hundred-year journey—at least—and we're going to look back in one hundred years and go, "Wow. The idea that you had to die at eighty or one hundred years 'old' makes no sense." Just like how today, going to Blockbuster Video makes no sense. What do you mean I have to get into a car and go all the way to a store where the movie might not be in stock *and* if it's not returned right away, I'll get charged extra? That is so bizarre. No, thank you. I think I'll stay on my couch and press this magic button that immediately delivers me *King Kong Battles Godzilla on Mars*.

At a certain point of innovation, the collective always clicks in and jumps on board. Like when the internet blew up or when everybody went out and bought a television. We're beginning to near that inflection point with human longevity and true health care. Change has never been more rapid, and information has never been easier to access.

Because we're not there yet, I still get a lot of pushback from people who don't understand what longevity is or what it means. A common response when I tell people what I'm working on is, "Oh, well. I don't want to live that long." People say this to me all the time. "Why would anyone want to live that long?"

Here's the thing people have to understand. When someone says, "You're going to live to two hundred," and you don't picture yourself healthy and happy, climbing mountains, living out your dreams, and all that jazz, you're missing the point. The vision that some of you have in your heads of living into what we currently call "old age" of grey-haired and hunched-over centenarians with barely enough energy to blow out the candles—that is not it. Human longevity isn't about living a decade or two extra marked by waning health. Human longevity means living at age twenty-two (or thirty-two or forty-two or whatever the ideal age is for you) in perpetuity: strong, healthy, moving freely, and thriving for the entire duration of your life. Human longevity means reaching our fullest potential and staying there. When you picture yourself at two hundred as some hunched over, greying, in-need-of-a-daily-diaper-changing version of what you understand aging to be, you're plugged into the old paradigm.

Obviously, nobody wants that! The "why would anyone want to live that long" reaction just goes to show you how ingrained the belief is that aging must be painful and miserable—because that's all it's ever been. Consider this: if someone from the birth records office called you up today to say, "Oh, there's been a mistake, you were actually born ten years earlier than you thought, so now you're going to die ten years sooner," would you really be okay with that? Would you just accept it because that's *just the way things are*?

Honestly. At what point do you become okay with your body degrading and falling apart? When will you be content with your cells turning cancerous and your eyesight failing you? At which juncture will you be happy about losing your hearing or struggling to walk around the block because of your aching back and hips and knees? If you're okay with any of those things happening to your body, that's your prerogative. But if you, like me, would rather keep your body as it is—or dare I say, you would rather live your life with more energy, clarity, and vitality than ever before—then we're ready to talk. Because then you, like me, have come to understand that we only believe we're supposed to die at a certain age because we have a social agreement that it's true.

What's actually true is that if you can conceptualize something in your mind *and* the science and technology are there to back up this visionary potential *and* you have some resources and the ability to follow through on your vision, then nothing is impossible.

Ask any Olympic athlete about the impossible. I don't think there's anybody out there who has made it to the Olympics who, as a child or youth, didn't spend incredible amounts of time envisioning and feeling fulfilled by the idea of going to the Olympics. They held the vision of the impossible in order to work through all the immense failure and disappointment and challenges that come with pursuing greatness. And when they succeeded, it was because they never let go of that vision. Like my work with electric cars. I didn't get into building electric cars because everyone else was doing it. I did it because I believed in it, despite the fact that almost no one else was doing it. I had a vision and a dream and a goal, and I pursued it despite everybody telling me I was crazy—that I was attempting to achieve the impossible.

Humans, innovators, artists, and scientists are always pushing the boundaries of the "impossible." Consider powered flight. That's something people once upon a time thought was impossible. They'd say, "Oh, if man were meant to fly, he'd have been born with wings," brushing off or calling crazy the daring minds who built the groundwork for air travel to take off. Anyone who claims something is impossible is just showcasing a lack of imagination. Even today, I have debates with people who argue that electric airplanes are never going to be viable. Meanwhile, electric airplanes transport people from A to B every day.

Dealing with pushback is the reality of every entrepreneur and innovator. Failure, rejection, rebuffs, and dismissals are part of the job. If your idea is truly revolutionary, you will get pushback. You just know that the first person to grab fire and start playing with it, the curious innovator who changed the human species forever, was almost certainly shunned and yelled at by people who said, "Leave that thing alone!"

People fear what they don't understand. That's a part of human nature. The part we must overcome. If you have a vision and can see a pathway forward for that vision, you must follow it.

Human lifespans have been lengthening for centuries. Now it's simply just a matter of exactly when we'll hit the tipping point where our expected lifespans increase faster than our increasing age. My parents are already decades beyond the life expectancy assigned to them at birth, and when I was born, the life expectancy for men was just eight years older than my current age. Yet today, I am healthier than I've ever been before and, by present day conventional standards, I am expected to live at least twenty more years.

So, when we're talking about longevity science and living beyond two hundred years old—with the health of a twenty-two-year-old—and you tell me that I'm out of my mind? I'll tell you that yes, I am out of the part of my mind that fixates on the "impossible," the past, and the notion that things have to stay the way they are or the way they've been. I'll tell you that I am firmly planted in the vision of what's possible: a better and brighter future for all of us.

Longevity is about living a fuller, happier, healthier life every single day. That's the real goal: improving the present and living longer with more vitality, stamina, and purpose. By focusing on making life richer and more enjoyable today, we'll sail into two hundred and beyond, thriving and enjoying all that Earth—and the cosmos—have to offer. It simply starts with taking intentional steps forward each day, taking better care of our bodies right now, and giving ourselves the tools we need to thrive. From there, we turn to the incredible scientific advancements underway.

"Aging is, quite simply, a loss of information." Those words from Dr. David Sinclair, author of *Lifespan*, make curing aging sound easy. But the truth of the matter is that the human body is incredibly complex. Fortunately, while most scientists will tell you that there's more that *we don't know* than *we do know*, humans continue to learn about ourselves at an astounding rate. And thanks to the growing field of longevity medicine, in recent decades our understanding around human aging has expanded exponentially.

There are many different theories on why we age and all sorts of angles and approaches that scientists have taken in attempting to understand what causes our bodies to degrade and die. One of the leaders in the field—and the author of the book *Lifespan: Why We Age and Why We Don't Have To*—is David A. Sinclair, PhD, a researcher and professor of genetics at Harvard Medical School. You may already be familiar with his work, but if you're not (and you don't have the time to pick up his book), there are numerous YouTube videos and podcasts you can check out to get an overview. Sinclair has quickly become one of the most familiar faces of the longevity conversation, not only for his research but also for his willingness to experiment with anti-aging medicine and technology on himself and his family.

Collecting his research and insights under the "Information Theory of Aging," Sinclair believes that we age because our cells lose information. The concept is pretty straightforward. Sinclair suggests that it's the wear and tear on our cells that causes damage to our genome and epigenome, essentially scrambling the information the cells need to continue functioning properly. Whether it's from not getting enough sleep, drinking too much alcohol, environmental factors like pollution or job stress, inherited biological factors, or otherwise, when our cells lose information, they can no longer replicate properly and they start misbehaving. This looks like cells multiplying into cancer, cells changing from skin cells to hair cells (yes, that's why you get hair sprouting out of weird places as you age), and cells turning into senescent "zombie" cells that create inflammation and general dysfunction that leads to disease and death.

Sinclair says that it is this loss of information—of damage over time—that causes us to age, not anything inherent to the makeup of the cell itself. As legendary physicist Richard Feynman said and as quoted at the top of this chapter, "There is nothing in biology yet found that indicates the inevitability of death. This suggests to me that it is not at all inevitable and that it is only a matter of time before biologists discover what it is that is causing us the trouble." It's been many years since Feynman uttered that statement, and today, scientists are closer than ever to having a full picture of what, indeed, is causing us all the trouble.

If you're familiar with Sinclair's work, longevity health at the cellular level, or biology at all, you know that aging is still considered to be a very complex process. You may have heard about sirtuins and telomeres and antagonistic pleiotropy and many of the other factors at play. Because I'm not a scientist, I recommend you dig into that research on your own, but I do want to give you a taste of what scientists believe is going on. The following is the best understanding I've gathered so far.

According to David Sinclair and many of his colleagues, epigenetic noise is the biggest reason why we age. Epigenetic noise is the damage that gets in the way of the epigenome properly reading the DNA, and that's when we see diseases, like aging, take over the body.

You can think about epigenetic noise like a broken smartphone screen and the contents of your phone as your DNA. Almost no matter what you do, your DNA will stay intact. It is digitally stored information that is very hard to damage. (Though it can develop mutations over a lifetime, overall it maintains itself very well like the good digital code it is.) But for the code to run properly, we need to be able to access it. If your phone's screen is damaged, you can't read the messages, open the apps you want, or make the right calls. While there's no problem with the apps and messages themselves—they're all there in the phone, good as new—it's the noise or shattered glass that is in the way. And the more noise or cracks in the screen, the more difficult it is to use your phone.

That's what smoking cigarettes, breathing in polluted air, drinking alcohol or contaminated water, undergoing a lot of stress, or not sleeping enough does to your cellular system: it makes little cracks on your screen. The only difference between you choosing which apps to open or messages to read, and your epigenome choosing which genes to turn on in your DNA, is that the epigenome is self-regulating and self-perpetuating, while *we* are making decisions moment to moment. (Then again, if you open TikTok automatically every time you can't sleep, you might be a little bit closer to the self-perpetuating epigenome after all!)

The epigenome is so, so important. It is the gatekeeper of the information that orchestrates all life—it is what tells the cells in our bodies, which are all genetically identical, to commit to and act out thousands of different roles. The epigenome is what tells a skin cell to be a skin cell and a heart cell to stay a heart cell rather than turn into a liver or brain cell. Without epigenetic information, our cells would lose their identities, and we'd quickly turn into a messy pile of mish mash mush. The epigenome shapes us into what we are. And noise, or damage, makes it difficult for it to do its job.

This is not to say that if you live a perfect life in a pristine environment away from damaging factors—i.e., you never scratch your phone—that you don't wear and tear in other ways. Because regardless of how well we take care of ourselves, the human body has certain built-in factors—components of our biological makeup—that change naturally over time. Meaning that keeping our cells healthy is not just avoiding smoking and alcohol and smoggy cities. It also means working with the biological trajectories within us that may be bent toward aging. These are additional factors that scientists must address as they explore how to stop us from degrading. The human body is complex.

That means that as we zero in, with more and more precision, on the exact specifics of how we're going to thrive beyond two hundred, we must remain humble to the unknown and curious to that which is currently beyond our scope of understanding. Fortunately, evolution's sole goal is to continue sustaining itself, which means the cards are in our favour. In fact, the cure for aging may be simpler than we can even imagine.

Picture yourself living on a quaint homestead back in the early eighteenth century. In this once upon a time scenario, you install a metal fence around your property to stop your animals from roaming away, and it works well for a while, but eventually your once-new, shiny metal fence succumbs to the environmental elements, like the sun and the wind and the rain, and breaks down. As the metal rusts away, you feel frustrated because it is time-consuming and expensive to replace, but you don't question it. Because *that's just the way things are.*

Or, that was just the way things were until somebody comes along (an Italian physician, physicist, biologist, and philosopher named Luigi Galvani) and figures out that when we galvanize and paint metal, it protects it from degradation. Suddenly, metal doesn't have to rust away anymore, and all it takes is a simple technique to treat the material. Now these fences can withstand the elements exponentially longer.

Up until today, humans have rusted away within seventy to one hundred years, all the while going along thinking "that's just the way it is." But this won't be the case for much longer. This is what we understand at Jevitty and what we're dedicated to helping others conceptualize: that there is enough science, enough gene therapy, enough stem cell therapy, and enough other technologies to galvanize ourselves so we don't have to rust away anymore.

Instead, we can look and feel, inside and out, like we were just installed. Good as new.

Some may argue that galvanizing our bodies to protect them from death and damage is somehow "unnatural" or "against nature," but then they would be forgetting that nature is constantly galvanizing itself against the elements in order to thrive better and longer. This is why we are alive and exist today. Life didn't peter out after single-celled organisms developed, though maybe it could have. Life instead chooses to evolve, to grow, to change, to move forward.

As you know, the human body is made up of trillions of cells. All living organisms are made up of cells—they are the most basic units of life. The number of cells in a living thing ranges from one (like with yeast) to quadrillions (like with some of the world's largest whales). Most cells are "differentiated," which means that they are set in their cell type and can't naturally change into something else. Stem cells are the cells with the potential to turn into different types of cells—they are the ones that can replenish us when our bodies have become damaged.

Cells come in all different shapes and sizes. Some can be seen by the human eye; for example, the yoke of a chicken egg is single cell, and the nerve cell that runs the entire length of our spine is one metre long. But most cells are so tiny that they can only be seen under a microscope—with most cells, you can fit ten of them across a single strand of hair.

Each cell has its own specific job. Some cells work on their own, but most cells work together. Common to all cells is making proteins (different from the protein you want to have on your plate at every meal) and producing energy—the energy that keeps us alive. Without our cells producing energy, we would be dead in a minute.

Cells have been around for more than a billion years, evolving over centuries and millennia to become stronger and more resilient. Today, cells are the powerful energy creators that keep us alive and allow us to thrive. Even though they are susceptible to damage, they are overall incredibly resilient. But it wasn't always this way. Once upon a time, cells were weak to the elements and wouldn't have been able to sustain human life. Because oxygen was harmful to their longevity, exposure to oxygen caused cells to corrode. That's right, folks. Prehistoric cells were prone *to rusting.*

Cells were weak and prone to rusting until a bacteria came along and joined forces with the cell. This was a match made in evolution heaven, creating the basis for all multicellular life. As Dr. Nir Barzilai, the founding director of the Institute for Aging Research at Albert Einstein College of Medicine, explains in his book *Age Later*:

> Cells have been on Earth for more than a billion years, but prehistoric cells existed in a crude form. These cells had low energy capacity and low function compared with the powerful cells we have today. And as if being low energy weren't enough of a challenge, the primitive cells were prone to corroding, or what we might call 'rusting,' thanks to oxygen in the environment. With so many challenges, the odds that these cells would amount to much were not good.
>
> But one day, a life-changing meeting occurred. A low-energy 'rust-prone' cell encountered a type of bacteria that didn't have much to brag about except that it happened to be very good at producing energy. Not only that, but the bacteria figured out how to defend against oxygen damage

by utilizing it for the energetic process. Unable to resist the bacteria's allure, the cell invited it in and enveloped it, and this was the start of a beautiful relationship between cells and the bacteria named *mitochondria*—it was the definition of symbiosis. Because of this union, cells became powerful, terrifically versatile, and adaptable. The cell had officially beaten the odds (122).

Isn't that incredible? Cells figured out how to galvanize themselves. Without that happening, none of us would be here today. What scientists are doing with longevity is an extension of this evolution. While humans now have a meta-awareness of our own evolution, the original directive hasn't changed: life works to sustain itself.

As society begins to understand the concept of human longevity, of conceptualizing aging as a disease, they'll be following behind the world's governments. In 2018, the World Health Organization (WHO) released the eleventh edition of the *International Classification of Diseases*, and in it, for the first time ever, they listed "aging" as a disease. This means, as Sinclair explains in his book, that at the beginning of 2022, countries had to begin reporting back to the WHO with statistics on citizens who died from aging as a condition. Talk about a paradigm shift.

We are in a time of exponential change. Innovation, often beyond comprehension, happens around the planet every day. Whether we measure it by the growth of artificial intelligence, the capacity of electric batteries, the proliferation of climate and ecological events, or by the advancements in longevity medicine and technology, we must admit that change is unfolding today at an unprecedented rate—and that it is staggering and often overwhelming to behold.

Tipping points are being activated everywhere. It's no longer reasonable not to believe in the "impossible." The time has come for big, bold visions and for our systems and structures, and society at large, to catch up with the progress and innovation happening all around it.

FROM SICK CARE TO HEALTH CARE

We are on the verge of a public
health breakthrough of the kind
we have never seen before.

S. Jay Olshansky

We live in a world where, every day, mechanisms beyond our control guide and shape our lives—whether it's advertisements telling us that "happiness" is a bottle of Coca-Cola or that "freedom" is an all-inclusive vacation; governments subsidizing oil and gas instead of funding clean innovation; news media blasting headlines of endless bad news instead of putting stories of positive breakthroughs at the top; or governments, again, gatekeeping mental and dental health care instead of ensuring free and accessible care for everyone—our life circumstances are dictated by numerous external factors, including factors that we might not even see or perceive.

I've often thought that if I could have asked my dog Zuka one question, it would have been, "What do you think is happening when we ride the elevator?" I was always curious to know about her level of understanding. Did she wonder about the mechanisms she couldn't see? Did she consider the world outside her immediate frame of reference? Did she feel awe? Or was she only ever thinking about her next bowl of food, never considering the magic occurring just out of her sight?

If Zuka and I stepped into an ioniser on Earth and stepped out on another planet light years away, would she even blink? Her nose would certainly register the different smells of this new place, but would she have any clue about the incredible technology that got us there? Would she understand that something truly significant had happened? Or would she be just as nonchalant as when we stepped out on the ground floor and trotted outside?

Dogs these days generally have pretty cushy lives. They don't need to worry about anything beyond the proximity of their favourite humans—there's no higher level of understanding required to survive. Some people may share this feeling of survival needs being met, leading them not to question the governing systems and structures that shape their lives. If you have access to private health care, have come to terms with and are comfortable with dying, and believe that you won't live long enough to be affected by the effects of climate change (like more pandemics, catastrophic weather events, the food chain breaking, or social collapse), then you are probably one of those people. For the rest of us, no matter how much privilege or positionality we have, when we observe the state of the world, we know that we can do better.

While nearly everyone understands the urgency of the energy shift needed to combat the climate crisis, and many understand the necessity of shifting our economic reality to one that eradicates poverty, only a few are currently talking about the shift needed in our health care system. Where I live, in Canada, because our health care system is more accessible than many places in the world, people give it significant praise. While I'm not saying that Canada's health care system doesn't deserve accolades, I am saying that we can do so much better. Our health care system may have some advantages, but we have to recognize that every health care system, everywhere in the world, is insufficient. Because these systems are overwhelmingly focused on sick care, not health care.

What I mean when I say that health care systems are overwhelmingly focused on sick care is that they are largely built on the premise of addressing acute health care issues like heart attacks, cancers, infections, traumas, viruses, and so on. Broadly speaking, acute conditions occur suddenly, have immediate or rapidly developing symptoms, and are limited in their duration. While acute care is definitely critical to treat and address, most of the health issues facing people today are not acute care issues but chronic health issues. Chronic conditions are long-lasting—which means they develop and potentially worsen over time. Of course, these diagnoses are not necessarily fixed. Acute conditions can become chronic, while chronic conditions may suddenly present with acute symptoms. They are separate and intertwined. The point I'm trying to make is that our health care system is built around helping people *after* they get sick instead of helping people *before* they get sick. As one of Jevitty's doctors has explained to me, "We've placed the ambulance at the bottom of the cliff. What we need to do is build barriers to stop people from falling off the cliff in the first place."

If you have a trauma, our health care system is awesome. This is the ambulance at the bottom of the cliff. Say you get hit by a bus—there's an amazing team of doctors that can put you back together and restore your health. Acute health care has also worked very well for infections and things that are temporary. Acute health care isn't going anywhere because traumas and infections aren't going anywhere—at least not yet. We need that ambulance at the bottom of the cliff. But at the same time, we need to broaden our health care system to also prioritize chronic health care, which our current health care system does not pay enough attention to.

Heart disease is the number one killer. It is a chronic condition overwhelmingly impacted by lifestyle. Since our health care system is focused on treating the end game of heart disease—acute symptoms like heart attacks—it misses the opportunity to support lifestyle changes that could reverse chronic conditions and prevent a heart attack from ever happening.

While we've been doing a lot better on heart disease over the last thirty or forty years, a big part of that is because, as a society, we've stopped smoking. Giving up smoking is a lifestyle choice and what we call proactive health care. By educating people on the dangers of smoking, we have placed a barrier on the side of the cliff. (Keep in mind, the cost of that railing is pennies compared to the ambulance fees at the bottom of the drop. It's also an industry consolidator, reducing the need for all sorts of businesses and services.)

Progress on heart disease has been incredible—between a dramatic reduction in smoking, developments with blood pressures medicines, and individual lifestyle changes to manage cholesterol, our current health care system has done a pretty decent job in terms of preventing or slowing chronic heart disease. The outcomes are far better than they were just a few decades ago, and the models for preventive cardiology are getting better every year. Our excellent acute system addresses severe outcomes of heart disease, and our chronic care system, including lifestyles changes, has lessened the overall impact of the disease.

Meanwhile, progress on cancer has been mixed. Cancer has been much harder to treat. While some of the new technologies and approaches have been game-changing, overall, we haven't seen wins on the war on cancer as a whole. Part of that is because the causes behind cancer are complex, rooted in so many different things. The war on cancer will be won by winning a thousand battles across all sorts of areas.

While we've seen success with heart disease and progress with cancer, our overall metabolic health has deteriorated dramatically. This is the biggest failure of our current health care systems. Metabolic health is lifestyle driven, meaning that the underlying roots of metabolic disease are found overwhelmingly in an individual's day-to-day behavioural choices.

One example of this is the prevalence of type 2 diabetes. In Canadians, type 2 diabetes is up from 2% in 1970 to 10% in 2022. Meanwhile, up to 70% of the population has some degree of insulin resistance, which means they're on the path to potentially becoming diabetic (Byrne). While our genetics haven't changed, our lifestyle choices clearly have.

Addressing metabolic health is something that we don't need fancy technology for. What we need is a paradigm shift around our lifestyles—and our approach to our overall health. Obviously, it's not just individual lifestyle change but also societal change that is required because we are driven by a food system where 50% of the calories that Canadians eat come from ultra-processed foods (Byrne), and those ultra-processed foods tend to lead toward obesity, which is the driving factor underlying type 2 diabetes. There are so many messages being pumped out into mainstream society, day after day, around eating crappy foods—foods that make us sick. We need a health care system that addresses the proliferation of this kind of marketing and advertising. It will be much more affordable for us in the long run. And it will save lives.

In a 2022 paper, researchers at the University of Alberta pegged the economic burden of excessive sugar consumption in Canada—that is to say, the direct and indirect costs of sixteen chronic metabolic diseases related to sugar—at $5 billion a year. Principal investigator Paul Veugelers released a statement with the paper that said, "Health care costs for chronic diseases are ballooning. We not only need to make our health care system more efficient, but we should also act on the demand side by investing in primary prevention to ensure we have fewer patients with chronic diseases. Addressing sugar consumption is one strategy to achieve that" (Rutherford). The researchers go on to call on the government to use "taxation, subsidies, education, and other measures to encourage healthier eating habits," underlining the urgent need for action.

You can see the parallel here to poverty and a universal basic income. By addressing problems at the root cause, we save our-selves money in the long run. By taking *preventative* action instead of reactive action, we build a base for everyone to have the chance to thrive (and live beyond two hundred!).

We can do so much more at community, social, and governmental levels to embrace and foster healthier lifestyles. Like better empow-ering individuals to make healthy choices. A big part of this will be helping people recognize that the food industry, by and large, hasn't been very helpful—that many food providers have been actively working against our better health and lifestyle. When we understand how marketing and advertising shapes behaviour, we arm ourselves with better tools to combat unhealthy cravings.

That said, lifestyle change is hard, right? Because the defaults are against you. From the pandemic to inflation and rising food costs to war and climate change, there's a lot to be stressed out about. Add on top of that, the marketing and advertising driven to tell you that you'll be "happier" if you eat this food or that food (and they're right about that too, at least temporarily, because the food gives you a momentary boost of energy). This is a big part of why we've created Jevitty—to help people with their behavioural change—to help support, incentivize, and motivate individuals to take the control back over their health and lifespan. The better we take care of our bodies, the slower we age, and the healthier we become.

So, let's help you understand your metabolic system a little bit better by looking at how your body processes sugar, in the hopes that this information will help you make more informed choices for your longevity. Considering that type 2 diabetes is such a rampant issue, I think many of us could use these insights.

The cells in our body primarily run on glucose, a simple sugar broken down from the carbohydrates we eat. While this is the body's primary source of energy, our cells can also run on fats or, if needed, proteins.

When we eat, food gets broken down into glucose and absorbed into our bloodstream. Insulin, which you're probably already familiar with, is the hormone that our body produces to regulate the amount of glucose in the blood. When we eat, the pancreas releases insulin in order to help transport the glucose into the cells, where it is converted into the energy that keeps us alive.

If you have normal blood sugar, there's only about one tablespoon of glucose in your blood at a time. But if you go and have, say, a massive sugary drink, you end putting in upwards of twenty times more glucose into your bloodstream than your body can process. What happens then is that the body wants to get rid of that glucose quickly because it's sticky—it's toxic.

Think about if you spilled a sugary drink on a table. That table would get sticky, right? That stickiness also happens inside the body. The glucose will stick to things and damage proteins, leading to diseases and other problems you don't want to happen. An overconsumption of glucose, as well as a sedentary lifestyle, are the leading factors behind type 2 diabetes.

When we eat too much sugar, what happens is our bodies convert a lot of it into fat (because we can't store it all in our limited storage space) and end up with higher levels of insulin in order to convert that glucose into stored fat instead of energy. This is problematic because high levels of insulin create the potential for insulin resistance. If we're constantly eating significant amounts of sugar, our insulin receptors stop working as well.

The best way to think of insulin is as an energy storage hormone as it not only packs glucose into our cells but fat into our fat cells. If we eat more than we can use at that moment, our body turns it into fat to use for a future day. Unlike the glucose storage system where the storage is limited, we have an almost unlimited ability to store fat. Fat, when stored safely, becomes a buffer for our body to use as extra energy.

Each one of us has a different threshold for healthy fat, meaning how much fat we can store safely, and by the age of eighteen, we're pretty much set in terms of the number of healthy fat cells we have. A safe place to put the fat is in the subcutaneous cells in your hips and butt. Though we can pack more fat into those cells, at a certain point they do become full and start to leak fat. And then what ends up happening is you start to get fat in places where it's not healthy, like the belly. When you start to see belly fat, that also means that you're likely starting to see fat within the liver, within the muscles, and within the pancreas. And fat in those areas makes those cells insulin resistant.

It's fat in the cells that causes the real problem with insulin resistance. When we're taking in too many calories, we're storing them as fat, but we're not storing them safely anymore because we're in energy overload, and that's when they start to muck up the system. This is where a vicious cycle kicks in. If the fat's driving the insulin resistance, it's going to push up insulin levels, and when insulin doesn't work as well, you need more insulin. And when you have higher levels of insulin, not only do you continue to push fat into storage, but you also stop the body's ability to burn and use fat. You get this sort of fat turnstile where fat can go in but can't come out. And that's what you see with insulin resistance—people get caught in this vicious cycle. After they eat, their insulin levels are so high they can't access the fat, so they get hungry again. It seems like it makes no sense because they've got lots of energy on board, but they get hungry again, so they eat more, and that just makes it worse. That drives a lot of the obesity that we see, which weighs heavily—no pun intended—on the health care system.

So, how do we reverse this cycle? Fortunately, the good people out there are on it! My friend, Dr. Brendan Byrne, has created a guide with his Lifestyle Rx 4+2 Diabetes Reversal Strategy, outlining the easy steps anyone can take to regain their autonomy and longevity.

The first step is to **Eat to Lower Insulin.** The simplest way to take the load off the pancreas is by decreasing the fast carbs that trigger insulin release. Choosing slow carbs with lots of fibre will lower insulin release and begin to break the metabolic "vicious cycle" of insulin resistance.

Next, make sure to **Use Your Muscles**. Increased exercise helps reverse insulin resistance, the process underlying type 2 diabetes, by improving glucose uptake and fat burning, even in the absence of weight loss. Exercise restores the muscles' role as an energy buffer for carbohydrates.

Now that you're eating right and moving your body, be sure to **Be Kind to Your Liver**. Fat in the liver is the biggest driver of insulin resistance and high insulin levels. When reversing insulin resistance, it is vital to ensure that the effect of energy overload is not compounded by factors that directly add fat to the liver—especially alcohol and fructose. Poor gut health and the resulting inflammation are also an often-overlooked root cause of liver inflammation and fatty liver. Our focus is on eliminating ultra-processed foods, decreasing alcohol, increasing fibre, and adding fermented foods to the diet.

Once that's on its way, it's time to **Restore Fat Burning**. The first three steps set the stage for this. To reverse insulin resistance and type 2 diabetes, you have to get rid of the fat in your liver and pancreas. To do this, you need to lose weight. Our preferred method for weight loss is time-restricted eating: limiting the number of hours we eat and extending the fasting period.

All along the way, it's pivotal to **De-Stress** and **Improve Sleep**. Stress can worsen insulin resistance and impede the reversal of diabetes. High levels of cortisol, the stress hormone, counteract many of insulin's actions while also increasing appetite. Improving stress tolerance helps by decreasing your stress reactions and improving your recovery from stress. Lack of sleep increases cortisol and appetite, so getting enough sleep is key to reversing insulin resistance and type 2 diabetes. Start by setting yourself up for a good night's sleep—give yourself at least an eight-hour sleep window and develop a sleep ritual to improve your sleep. If there are any signs or symptoms of obstructive sleep apnea, be sure to get a professional assessment and investigate what's impeding your rest and recovery time.

Your health is in your hands. Living and thriving until two hundred and beyond isn't about waiting around for some magic injection. It's about living your very best life right now.

Jevitty is committed to supporting and democratizing longevity by supporting and incentivizing individuals with their health goals and supporting and funding companies in their research and production. Dr. Byrne's Lifestyle Rx 4+2 Diabetes Reversal Strategy is just one of the many companies and endeavours we are supporting at Jevitty. We've already invested over half a million dollars in both private and publicly traded health companies all over the world, across different areas of interest.

As we'll learn in the final chapters, the changes ahead are astounding. Most of us are looking at the Grand Canyon through a toilet paper roll. What we're seeing may be accurate, but it is limited. We may not even properly comprehend what we're seeing because, without the context of the bigger picture, how can we really know?

In one hundred years, flight has gone from impossible to fully integrated into our daily lives. In a few decades, we've gone from computers the size of a room to computers fitting neatly in our pockets. Soon we'll see health care go from ambulances at the bottom of the cliff to drones in the air and sturdy fences at the edge. Change appears to be exponential. I hope you're feeling ready for the shift.

LONGEVITY ESCAPE VELOCITY

Longevity has gone from hope to promise.

Andrew Steele

Do you remember the old "double penny a day" adage? Someone probably taught it to you when you were a kid in order to illustrate the importance of patience and hard work, or to teach you about compounding interest. Maybe it was presented to you like this: Would you rather receive $5,000 or the amount of money that comes from starting with one penny and doubling it every day for a month? If you're a kid who hasn't learned about this concept, you'd probably go for the $5,000—one penny isn't much, and by day four you only have eight cents, so it doesn't seem like a good deal. But as soon as you understand how compounding works, this concept of exponentiality, you realize that you'd be missing out on exponential wealth. A penny a day, doubled for thirty days, adds up to $5 million by the end of the month.

That's one way to think about Longevity Escape Velocity (LEV): recognizing that by investing in our health and making good choices today, we're investing in our health for the exponential future. Essentially, the longer you live, *the longer you'll live.*

Let's say you decide to quit smoking. By committing to and follow-ing through with this decision, you're extending your predicted lifespan by at least ten years. Even if technology doesn't advance at all in that time, you've still added ten years to your life—and prob-ably more health and vitality in those years too. This is great on its own. But *with* velocity? You're not just adding ten years—you're adding ten years plus all the medicines and advancements that come on board in that time.

All this velocity adds up to the potential of infinite more years. Because technology is advancing so quickly, taking action to safe-guard your health and improve your vitality today allows for your health and vitality to compound over time. This snowball effect tells us that we have the potential to cross the threshold into the next stage of human life: living forever.

The purpose of Jevitty is to support this mission. To give people the tools, tricks, technology, and insights they need to achieve LEV. What Jevitty is here to do is to support you in achieving the fullest and most vital life you can live *right now*, and in doing so, safeguarding yourself so that you're best protected for the future. Because no one wants to die a month before scientists release the anti-aging vaccine, right?

The Jevitty app will be the windshield to your car, the dashboard to your spaceship. Kind of like how Tesla monitors your car while you're driving so they can tell you to come in if something is about to go wrong. When you get the ping from Tesla, it happens *before* you're stranded on the side of the road, right? This is pro-active, lifestyle-driven health care. Jevitty will do its part to help you before you have the heart attack or the stroke or the cancer, giving you the little service pings: "Hey. There's something going a bit wrong. Why don't we find a way to course correct it before anything gets worse?" Can you imagine how dramatically this will shift the health care paradigm and society at large?

At Jevitty, we take a five-level approach to LEV, kind of like the five levels to autonomous driving. At the beginning, we're just testing things out, giving up some of our vices in exchange for the health of our future selves. Then, step by step, we go along the way to the fifth level, where suddenly there's not even a steering wheel.

As David Sinclair explains in *Lifespan*: "DNA monitoring will soon be alerting doctors to diseases long before they become acute. We will identify and fight cancer years earlier. If you have an infection, it will be diagnosed within minutes. If your heartbeat is irregular, your car seat will let you know. A breath analyzer will detect an immune disease beginning to develop. Keystrokes on the keyboard will signal early Parkinson's disease or multiple sclerosis" (213). With the advancement and proliferation of tools like smart watches and health monitoring rings, doctors have more and more accurate information about their patients, and proactive health care will become a completely normal part of our lives.

Our goal is to reach peak health and stay there without having to think about it. Cruise control, if you will. With Jevitty, we help you reach the gold standard of health and support you in sustaining it until good health practices become second nature.

The **Five Levels of Longevity Escape Velocity** are straightforward. They're all very doable, especially once you have the purpose piece in place—which we will talk more about later in this chapter— because, as we know, it's tough to take care of your health if you're not in a good headspace.

The first step to LEV is to **Reduce Risk**. This means cutting out the things that harm your health, like smoking cigarettes, throwing back martinis with abandon, eating junky food—that sort of reckless behaviour. Level one is eliminating and cleaning up that stuff, removing the behaviours that are harmful to your health.

The next step, the second level of LEV, is to **Increase Health and Slow Aging**. Now that you've reduced or eliminated harmful behaviours, it's time to optimize the beneficial stuff like sleeping properly, adequately exercising several times a week, eating good food, fasting at least twelve hours between dinner and break-fast, and so on. Step one bleeds into step two, of course. They're all intertwined. You remove the McDonald's and replace it with organic, seasonal foods. You limit screen time before bed so you're not tossing and turning and struggling to fall asleep. You replace your smoking habit with a mindfulness meditation. You get the picture. It'll get easier as you go, especially as good habits form. Soon you'll be waking up with more vitality and excitement as you see the compounding effects of all the good ways you've been taking care of yourself.

Step three of Longevity Escape Velocity is **Age Cessation**. This is where the more medicinal and technological pieces come in to stop the aging process altogether. This is mRNA stem cells, telo-mere technology, gene therapy … technologies, medicines, and interventions that will stop the process of aging, repair biological functions, and rejuvenate your physical body.

LEV's fourth step is to **Return to and Maintain Peak Age**. This is where we roll back the clock until we hit our peak health. Directly tied into the third step, many of the medicines and technologies we'll use to stop aging will be the same technologies we use to reverse aging and maintain our ideal age. I suspect that within the next five years, we'll have access to mRNA technology that will be able to do things like regenerate the liver and the blood, bringing you back to the health level of a twenty-two-year-old.

You might be wondering what could possibly be left once you're not smoking or drinking, you're sleeping like a champion, and you're as healthy as a horse with a VO$_2$ of forty-five, the energy of a twenty-two-year-old, and the purpose of someone who knows that they're going to be alive and exploring and innovating for as long as they so choose. What more could you possibly want?

Even though we've figured out how to stop aging, there is still danger in the world and there are still ways your lifespan could be shortened or, heaven forbid, ended. The fifth and final stage of Jevitty Longevity Escape Velocity is to **Maximize Life.** The app will monitor your day-to-day activities to make sure you're not unknowingly doing anything that will put you in harm's way, showing you how and where you can reduce risk of accidents with the help of the algorithm that will look for harm outside of your physical or psychological control. It doesn't matter if you're eighteen or eighty, the math is the same if you get hit by a truck. Until or unless we develop some Star Trek–level healing tools, we want to avoid that kind of damage to our bodies.

For example, say you walk to work at 8:30 a.m. every morning. The algorithm will look at all the car accidents on your route between the hours of 7:30 and 9:00 a.m., crunch the numbers from the past fifteen years, and spit out the safest time for you to be on your way. Maybe it will tell you it's safer to walk at 8:45 a.m., so you decide to leave fifteen minutes later to reduce risk and enjoy a more pleasant, less traffic-filled walk.

Even though this is the final stage, it will probably kick in before we fully accomplish stages three and four. There's no reason to wait to reduce risk, right? That's why all the stages work with and inform each other. Just think of everything that you'll learn about yourself on the way. You'll discover new layers of yourself you never even knew were there, while deepening into the fullest version of yourself.

The key to this process, like anything else, is balance—maintaining a healthy perspective so you can make Longevity Escape Velocity fun.

Some of the Best Things You Can Do to Lock in Longevity Escape Velocity

Sleep

Sleep is *so* important. While researchers have struggled to nail down an exact correlation between sleep length and longevity (because there are so many other factors that contribute to a person's health that affect the amount of sleep one gets each night, like stress and underlying disease, for example), we do know that when we sleep, our brains flush out toxins (in particular the toxic amyloid, which is implicated with Alzheimer's disease). Sleep also helps regulate your metabolism, strengthens your immune system, and helps relieve the stress you accumulate throughout the day.

I'm fortunate that I've always been a good sleeper; that's never been a struggle for me. Except, on occasion, when something is really bugging me. If I wake up in the middle of the night thinking about a work problem, say something the finance guys are doing, that's when I know the situation must be addressed immediately. For me, I know that poor sleep is not about my body's *ability* to get a good sleep but about environmental factors that needs to be addressed. A sleepless night is my subconscious talking to me.

My primary goal with sleep is to close all the rings on my sleep app. I'm always looking for a minimum of eight hours. If I don't get eight hours, then the ring on the app I use stays yellow. Once I'm at eight hours, the app turns green, and if I go to nine hours or above, it turns purple, which is excellent.

I'm not the only one who loves sleep. Some of the greatest athletes of all time advocate for over nine hours of sleep a day. Did you know that LeBron James has said he sometimes sleeps up to twelve hours a day? At minimum he wants eight to ten hours a night, and he says that if people call him lazy, he'll tell them off. Sleep helps him to be ready for everyone and everything—his teammates, his family, his sponsors—he needs to show up for, and there's nobody more ready than Lebron James.

Lebron is not the only athlete who's made headlines for committing to a healthy and hefty sleep schedule. Roger Federer apparently gets around ten to twelve hours each night, and athletes like Gabby Douglas, Usain Bolt, and Michael Phelps have all spoken up about the benefits of getting a good and long night's sleep.

There are certain things you can do to improve sleep hygiene: no screens before bed, take a warm bath, read a calming book, listen to calming music or sounds, or do a meditation. Getting a better sleep could even be as simple as stopping drinking caffeine fifteen to thirty minutes earlier than you usually do or adjusting your bedroom temperature; a cooler sleeping environment can often be supportive, as can reducing light and noise pollution as much as possible.

Oftentimes, the people who can't sleep don't try these things, preferring to toss and turn into the wee hours. Sometimes people will use alcohol to help them sleep, which can do a good job of knocking you out when you first lie down, but it's going to disrupt your sleep over the long term and can also cause you to wake up in the middle of the night.

While I don't know much about the science of dreams, many researchers insist that spending time asleep and dreaming is important for our cognitive health, and who doesn't want more time to dream up our next adventures and BHAGs? Besides, if we're living forever, why not sleep twelve hours a night? It's not like we have to worry about wasting daylight anymore. That stuff is infinite.

Intermittent Feasting

There are *a lot* of opinions out there about intermittent fasting and caloric restriction. In longevity research, across the board, restricting calories is the most sure-fire way to extend one's lifespan. Caloric restriction shows the best results for slowing aging in yeast, mice, humans, and many, many other creatures. Why? Because of autophagy—which means giving our cells an opportunity to rejuvenate themselves. Intermittent feasting is not about painful restriction or starvation. Getting enough nutrients is just as key as giving your cells time to clean and repair themselves.

That's why I prefer to call this longevity technique intermittent *feasting*. Time restricted eating without thinking about the nutritional or enjoyment side of things is pointless. We're not living longer to be miserable, are we? Intermittent feasting allows you to enjoy your food *more* instead of less. Eating less overall should and can translate into more enjoyment. If you keep the feasting to a smaller amount of time than the fasting, then you're pretty much set.

While metrics are great starting points (of which you'll find hundreds of different interpretations and opinions in books and online), adapting the metrics to your body's specific needs is key. Obviously, we're not going to overdo it in the feasting window, nor are we going to make poor choices that reduce our vitality. But we're also not going to worry about counting calories because we know we're tackling the most important part by giving our bodies a break to rest in between feasts. Metrics can and should shift with you as you grow and change as a human being. The more our health care system becomes personalized to individuals, the easier this will become.

One popular fasting metric is 16/8: 16 hours of fasting with an 8-hour window for eating. This metric works well for some people, and it may work well for you some of the time. I usually keep my feasting between 8:00 a.m. and 4:00 p.m., but if my wife, who works later hours, comes home and says, "Let's share a meal," I will join her. Because that's fun, right? We're not living longer to punish ourselves. That's why I'm not super strict about my feasting window. Everything in moderation, including moderation, right?

David Sinclair, our friendly neighbourhood researcher, recently explained on his podcast that he eats one meal a day (a technique referred to as "OMAD"). This is a reduced amount from when he wrote his book and explained that he only tried to skip one meal a day. Now he'll eat a significant amount in a short amount of time, and he says he's never felt better. That might work for him, but it can generally be difficult to get enough nutrients, especially enough protein, in that short amount of time.

The most important thing I've learned about intermittent fasting/ feasting is to keep my blood sugar levels regulated. As we learned earlier, insulin resistance is a huge problem and a huge detriment to our health. Often people will think they're hungry, but actually, it's just their blood sugar crashing. Our bodies can only process so much glucose at once. If you're eating food that spikes and then crashes your blood sugar, of course you're going to need to eat more. If we take in more than we can handle, we're messing with our metabolic system. Once you've regulated your blood sugar, your fasting hours will become a breeze. Then it's just the emotional or habitual impulses to eat that you'll have to deal with. Once you overcome those, you'll realize that you're not as hungry all the time as you thought you were.

You can use a flash or continuous glucose monitor, you could start a food journal, or you could just start paying close attention to how you feel after eating rice, bread, potatoes, chicken, veggies, pastries, etc. They all affect our bodies differently, and it's up to you to understand what works best for you and what will keep your body nourished and regulated.

Remember that if your insulin level is high, you could starve yourself and still not lose any weight. If your insulin level is out of whack, it doesn't matter how much exercise you're doing, your body is not reacting properly. You have to get your insulin levels in check so that your body can receive glucose and burn it off properly.

Nutrition

I'm a big fan of waffles. They're pretty much my favourite thing. I asked my nutritionist about my habit and they said that optimally, I'd be eating avocado, eggs, and kale or something similar for breakfast, as opposed to a waffle—or multiple waffles, with custard. They did say that if it was a whole wheat waffle, that would be a bit better. Either way, it's still a sugar that's harder on my metabolism than veggies and protein.

I used to eat waffles two to three times a week, but now I only eat them a couple of times a month, and I generally save them for occasions when I'm meeting up with friends and can really revel in the whole experience. That's why I find the easiest thing for me to do in regard to keeping my nutrition on track is the 80/20 rule. I've heard this from a lot of people, including Dwayne "The Rock"

Johnson. For 80% of the time, I make sure I'm avoiding simple carbs and sugars and focusing on vegetables and protein, and then the other 20% of the time, I eat my fruit waffle with custard. And enjoy the hell out of it.

I'm not strict with myself about nutrition. I make sure my ship is orientated in the right direction and I don't worry about the rest. I don't sit there measuring stuff out or counting calories. That's not sustainable, and the goal is to have a sustainable life—to *enjoy* life. The other day, I was getting ready to go out for a run at eight o'clock in the morning, and my wife said, "Hey, do you want to go have breakfast at Granville Island Hotel this morning?" I almost told her, "No, I'm going to go for a run. I'll see you later." But then I went, *You know what. Screw that. Let's go for eggs benedict.* And when you think about it, that's just a smarter thing to do. To live in the moment and accept invitations for joy and connection and community. But the key is to make sure you don't feel guilty. You have to feel good about yourself and the choices you make. And that will make it a lot easier to commit to eating kale and veggies later in the day. And while you're watching your glucose intake, it's also great to remember to get protein and fibre on your plate at every meal.

To support myself further, I take a handful of supplements five days a week. My doctor has told me that giving my body a break from the supplements on weekends is a good thing, that it makes them more effective in the long run. I take vitamin B12 complex, two teaspoons of omega-3, 2000 IU of vitamin D with K2 (it's important to take K2 with your vitamin D to ensure that it's absorbed properly), quercetin, resveratrol, and niagen. I also take a product called Ocumetics, after having laser eye surgery about fifteen years ago, and a nightly probiotic.

None of this stuff is cast in stone. If one day new research comes out saying quercetin is bad for you, I'll stop taking it. We're always going with best practices we know at the time. And if things need to change, we trust that little adjustments over a long period of time will have the biggest positive effect. Remember, orient your ship in the right direction and don't fall into the trap of swinging the steering wheel too hard to the other direction. Small course corrections can dramatically change the trajectory of our journey over time. Oftentimes, that's all we need to stay on the right track.

As for alcohol, I'll have a drink here and there at events or for celebrations, but overall, I'm not a big drinker. Though I do love Jägermeister. Growing up in a German household where Jägermeister was something you would drink once a day on the farm to warm your body up, there's still something really comforting in it for me. Drinking it makes me happy and makes me think of my family and Christmastime and all that fun stuff. Sure, there's different herbs and tinctures in Jägermeister that might benefit your physical health—though I don't know that they've done any studies on them. But having those one or two doses in a week does so much for my mood and attitude and improves my overall well-being. Whatever the medicinal effects are, it's also a psychological therapy for me.

The research on alcohol consumption is mixed. Every country has different recommendations. We know that overconsumption is definitely not good for us, but the bulk of the research suggests that moderate consumption can extend your lifespan. That said, the Canadian Centre on Substance Abuse and Addiction just changed their recommendation to zero drinks a week being the healthiest choice … Something to keep an eye on and an awareness of.

Ultimately with eating and nutrition, you must be kind to yourself and listen to your body. Sometimes your body feels like it needs more, and sometimes your body feels like it needs less. It's not going to always match up with some chart or calorie plan. (Also, it's been proven that our bodies retain calories differently depending on our stress levels, so stressing about how many calories you're eating can actually change the calorie count of your food!) If I'm full, I stop eating. If I'm still hungry, I'll make sure that I don't go to bed feeling miserable. Again, it's about sustainability and developing a clear relationship to what you actually need and not just what you feel an impulse for.

Whenever I feel like I'm not capable of achieving something, like regulating my eating to what my body truly needs instead of hitting the waffles every morning, it helps me to think about it like the ten and one marathon rule I learned from The Running Room, a wonderful organization in Canada that helps train people who want to run a marathon. It's simple: you run for ten minutes and then you walk for one minute. It's the loveliest thing because you've broken it down into ten-minute bites, which makes it so much more manageable. Instead of running for twenty or thirty minutes and giving up, you run for four or five hours with these tiny little reprieves in between.

It's like if I gave you a twenty-pound box of apples to see how long you could hold it. You could probably hold it for maybe twenty minutes, and then you'd have to put it down and you'd be done. But if I told you that every five minutes you could put the box down for a minute, you could probably hold it all day long. It's the same thing with food. Same thing with exercise. Same thing with sleep. Do your best, take breaks, and monitor your input/output so you're not primed to burn out.

Exercise

I run three to five days a week and strength train three days a week. It's hard work, which is why I exercise with friends as much as possible and work with a private trainer once a week. With my trainer, it's not just physical training. He looks at things like balance and flexibility as well as strength. Those are all vital components. We check in online, and as I'm doing bouncing and stretching and things like that, he's watching me and will say, "Oh, that was a little too challenging. Let's back off," or, "Hey, that was good. Let's up the challenge on that." It's ideal to have specific feedback and not just be on a broad program.

Sometimes I run by myself around the neighbourhood, but mostly I run with friends or my running coach, Carey Nelson. I also launched a meetup.com group, "The Vancouver Running and Jogging Club," that now has eight thousand members with about three or four different weekly running and socializing meetups. I attend as many as I can. It's a wonderful community. Since I've started it, many of my members have gotten married to each other and had children, which just goes to show how fun and engaging exercising can be. Running isn't just physical exercise—it's social.

Something I've been testing out is "slow running." Many doctors say that this is as close as you can get to waving a magic wand to build up lean body mass and get rid of the bad visceral fat: slow running first thing in the morning in what's called zone two—a little more intense than a warm-up but not intense enough that you're in the aerobic zone. You want to have your heart rate between 100 and 115, even if that means you're walking. For me it looks like 4.4 miles per hour on the treadmill for five to ten kilometres, so about a half-an-hour to an hour. I'll do this slow running in the morning before I break my fast.

The rest of my runs are more high intensity, usually ten to twenty kilometres with my coach and other friends. I just did a twenty-kilometre run with some of my crew, chatting the whole way, in one hour and fifty minutes. Not Olympic calibre by any means, but a solid, social run.

Generally, you don't want to run more than five days a week. Your probability of getting injured gets too high. Carey tells me that over his years of training people for marathons, even running three times a week can be sufficient practice. If you're running five kilometres three times a week, you're meeting and probably exceeding your longevity cardiovascular goals. If you're training, you're going to be doing significantly more than that. Carey recommends not running more than sixty-five kilometres a week, and to make sure you're also doing some strength training.

Strength training is particularly important for bone health and bone density. When we lift weights or do push-ups or other resistance training, we're causing a healthy strain between our muscles and our bones that strengthens them over time. Even small increments of weightlifting can make a huge difference in your overall health, and bone density is very important to stay on top of for longevity.

While strength training is for everyone, running isn't. There are all sorts of different ways to get your cardio in—even taking a brisk walk around the block (a great time to do this is after a big meal). You could do dance classes (YouTube is full of them, or you could find somewhere to attend in your community), hit the elliptical machine, go for a hike or a bike ride, or put on that VR headset and try out the latest fitness game. The important thing is finding exercise that you enjoy. The more you enjoy it, the easier it will be for you to do regularly. My favourite part of running is chatting with friends, but maybe you love catching up on the newest murder mystery podcast or DJ set list … Do what you need to do to get your heart rate up, even if it's just fifteen minutes a couple times a week. This will increase your VO_2 max and pay dividends for your Longevity Escape Velocity.

VO_2 Max

If you already have the Jevitty app or work with other health apps, you'll be familiar with VO_2 max. VO_2 max is the maximum (max) rate (V) of oxygen (O_2) your body is able to use during exercise. VO_2 max measures your body's ability to absorb oxygen and is a great indicator of the state of your health. You want a high VO_2 max so that your body can take more oxygen from the air and deliver it to your muscles and, in turn, your muscles can absorb more nutrients. Think about your VO_2 max like a fire that's burning inside of you. This fire protects your overall health. The bigger the fire and the hotter it's burning, the better you're going to be able to burn away any health issues that come your way. Say a virus comes knocking on your door—that's like throwing wet cardboard on the fire. If the fire's hot enough, it will burn away at wetness without a problem. But if the fire isn't very strong, the wet cardboard could snuff it out.

VO_2 max is one of the top things the Jevitty app looks at when it crunches the numbers on how long you could live. The higher the number, the more Longevity Escape Velocity you have. So how do you get your VO_2 max to go up? Cardio. Cardio. Cardio. High intensity exercise, interval training, and pushing yourself to new limits. At a reasonable pace, of course. It really doesn't take a whole heck of a lot to get up to a VO_2 max of about forty-five. Just consistent, dedicated effort over time. Now, forty-five is just an example. Everyone has a different ideal VO_2 max, even though the higher the better is a standard metric to go by. Ultimately, though, like everything else with longevity, you have to tailor it to your own unique body and life experience. The simple way to start is with easy but brisk walks.

Managing Stress

One of David Sinclair's top pieces of health advice in *Lifespan* is, "Don't sweat the small stuff," and I couldn't agree more. The goal of longevity is to make our lives richer and more enjoyable, which directly translates into reducing stress. Well, reducing the bad kind of stress, that is.

According to physiology, stress is a stimulation of the nervous system. It is the physiological response we have toward external or psychological stressors. When the human mind detects some kind of threat or challenge, it releases the stress hormones in the body: adrenaline and cortisol. For our ancestors, stress was a survival mechanism. In many ways, it still is today. Stress can tell us when we're in an unsafe situation and can reveal to us the places in our lives where we need to change our behaviour.

It can be challenging to talk about the concept of stress, since there are so many different kinds. For some people, working out and fasting can be stressful, but we now know that taking breaks between meals and breaking a sweat or exercising to the point that you're short of breath is really good for you. That kind of stress is what Dr. Sinclair calls "adversity memetics."

Then there's the stress of having to wake up early to catch a plane for an exciting trip or prepping to give a big talk on a topic you're passionate about. These experiences can release adrenaline and cortisol too, but they are also accompanied by other physical and psychological reactions. Since there are so many different ways to look at stress, it might be easier if we refer to the kind of stress that's good for us as "a-stress" and we talk about the kind of stress that's bad for us as "distress."

Distress is the emotional state a person encounters when they fail to adapt themselves to stressors. Distress can become a prolonged and compounding state of being. We want to avoid distress as much as possible. Distress can be very damaging to our health, whereas a-stress can improve our health significantly.

All the longevity insights we've discussed so far can help reduce distress in your life. Regular exercise, good nutrition, and sleep are all key factors in reducing compounding stress. However, it is possible that on the journey of integrating longevity techniques into your lifestyle, you may experience distress. Perhaps you tend to beat yourself up if you don't fast for "long enough," or you struggle to get enough exercise and get worked up trying to find the time to work out.

If you ever find yourself in a situation where, in the attempt to extend your longevity, you end up in a state of distress, please take a break and go easy on yourself. This is supposed to be fun and enjoyable. In the coming years and decades, as we nail down the age-halting and age-reversing processes, people are going to tell you all sorts of things that you "should" be doing to extend your longevity. Remember what's most important: commitment to the long-term, which means being happy and calm in the now while you implement and experiment with small, growth-orientated changes along the way.

If you're looking for ways to reduce your distress right now, meditation might be a good option for you. The science behind meditation is growing, and researchers continue to demonstrate how a mindfulness practice can greatly benefit many people's lives. Meditation can improve your sleep, increase your motivation to work out, improve your creative thinking skills, bolster your immune system, reduce chronic pain, reduce risk of heart attack, and, well, relieve stress in general. Resting in general or making time for silence or calming music is a great idea, especially in this day and age when we're constantly inundated with so much noise.

There are all sorts of ways people incorporate meditation or mediation—like activities in their lives. For you, that could look like taking long walks, lying in the grass or on the beach, putting away your phone for a few hours or even the whole day, cooking an elaborate meal, gardening, or any other number of things—it could be something as simple as taking off your shoes and socks and putting your bare feet on the earth. Heck, it might be cranking up the tunes and dancing it out! My wife, Naz, finds her zen in racing cars, believe it or not. You know best what calms you and allows your mind time to rest. And if you don't know what calms you, explore away. Spending time in nature is always a great place to start. Science has backed this up many times over the years, that going outside and spending time around trees and flowers will do your psyche good. And it's a good reminder of why we commit to our longevity—so that we may enjoy the many riches of the world around us.

Purpose

The three most important things that solve 99.9% of your health issues are getting a great sleep, eating great food, and getting a decent amount of exercise, and none of these happen unless you're in a good place mentally. If you're in distress or feeling frantic or scared, you do not have the psychological bandwidth to exercise or eat well. You're going to eat crappy food, have an upset sleep, and not have the energy to take yourself out for a run. Or, at the very least, it's going to be a struggle, and you're not going to be able to hit the same levels that you would if you were in a happy place, feeling good about the sun coming up each day, and dancing in the rain because you're in love with life. Good mental health, which is fostered and bolstered by purpose, is the umbrella over everything else.

Purpose is the unsung hero of the longevity movement. Purpose affects our lives in so many intertwining ways. We might even consider purpose to be the driving factor behind life itself. Purpose motivates us to exercise, eat well, go to bed at a decent hour, and reduces the likelihood of distress, all of which contribute to a longer lifespan. Purpose is what you make of it and can be as straightforward as choosing to spread love and kindness and choosing to find peace and contentment with what is.

Research shows that people who believe that their existence has meaning have lower levels of the stress hormone cortisol and more favourable gene expression related to inflammation, and a 2016 study published in *Psychosomatic Medicine* found that having a purpose in life can lower your mortality risk by about 17% (Zaraska). (This is information I learned from the "News" section of the Jevitty app, by the way!)

That is something for us all to consider. What motivates us? What keeps us going? What gives our lives meaning? What is our unique purpose, how does it drive us forward, and how do we foster, sustain, and allow our purpose to flourish?

IMMORTALITY AND BEYOND

*The idea that humans must live within
the natural environmental limits of our
planet denies the realities of our entire
history, and most likely the future.
Our planet's human-carrying capacity
emerges from the capabilities of our
social systems and our technologies more
than from any environmental limits.*

Erle C. Ellis

Once upon a time, great men and women dreamed about leaving a legacy. In dedicating their lives to making the world a better place, they wanted to make a mark on society and humanity so that their names might be remembered for generations to come. Today, we don't need to leave a legacy anymore because we don't need to leave. We will become living legacies, dedicated to making the world a better place not only for our great-great-grandchildren, but for us to enjoy with them.

Can you even imagine what it would be like to sit down with your great-great-great-grandparents? Or better yet, to have them over for dinner once a month? Imagine the wealth of knowledge that they could give to you. To be able to hear their stories and share in their wisdom, to learn all about where you came from, your family history and lineage, and to have their support in navigating your life today—one can only dream of how dramatically these relationships would affect our lives for the better.

Consider how much gets lost when someone dies. Allowing people to die is like burning a library of irreplaceable books. When you consider the depth and possibility of what human longevity means, of having the wisdom and knowledge of so many generations present on the Earth at the same time, it is truly breathtaking.

They say history repeats itself, but does it have to? I think about the rise of 45th President of the United States Donald Trump and my mother's reaction. My mom, who was a child during the Nazi regime, would call me up and say, "Jerry, this is happening all over again." She was so upset. At first, I didn't understand the gravity of the situation, but once she explained what she'd witnessed in her childhood, it hit me just how concerning Trump's behaviour was and is. My mother had a much deeper understanding than I did of what was going on because she'd experienced that history first-hand.

I hear that some people are concerned with older generations living longer and thereby stagnating progress. But this kind of thinking fixates on the negative and ignores the reality that it is faulty systems and unevolved human behaviour that keeps us stuck in bad positions. The truth is: longevity is happening, whether you like it or not. Our focus must be on innovating beyond our current problems instead of wasting our precious energy attempting to push back against the tide.

I promise you that a few short years after this book comes out, the potential of human longevity will be widely known. It is not long now before the evolution of the science and technology—and the evolution of our species—becomes undeniable. We've invented tools that we don't even fully comprehend yet. It's now up to us to learn how to keep up. Much of the technology is here. What's limited is the human ability to interpret and integrate it.

DNA methylation testing, for example. I've done it about fifteen different times with as many different companies. The results have been more or less accurate with my age—they usually land within about half a year of my chronological age—but the rest of the information they've provided has been disappointingly nebulous. I'll often do the testing with my wife, who is very different from me on the surface—she's of Persian descent, I'm of German descent, and there's a foot-and-a-half height difference between us—but with many tests, the results will come back exactly the same. That's when you know the human interpretation is lacking. We sniff that out quickly and don't use that service again. Sometimes they'll tell you things that are just unequivocally untrue. One hilarious test result said that genetically, I'm at a very low risk of losing my hair. We laughed and laughed when that one came back. I haven't needed a barber in twenty years. They couldn't have gotten it more wrong. You can't always rely on the interpretation of the information. If a genetic test comes back and it tells you to avoid coffee and blueberries, take it with a grain of salt.

Those aren't the only human error flubs I've had in health care over the years. About fifteen years ago, my general practitioner did a chest MRI on me right before I went off to run the Boston Marathon. Two weeks later I met with the doctor and he told me, "Well, we got the scan back from the lab, and the diagnosis from the MRI person is that you have COPD, an inflammatory lung disease." I just looked at him, flabbergasted, and he said, "Obviously, that's rubbish." It turns out, the lab tech had read the MRI completely wrong and reported back with false information, freaking both me and my physician out. There was nothing wrong with the MRI machine; it was just human interpretation that messed things up. My doctor called the lab back to inform them that the patient had just run a 3:10 marathon in Boston. No COPD, lungs are just fine, thank you.

For human longevity to click in, we need people who understand what the technology is saying. It's like in motorsports where you have these sensors all over the car—for the brakes, accelerator, steering wheel, G meters, strain gauges, and so on—and as you drive the car, the sensors record the statistics. Then, after the race, you download it onto a laptop and look at all the graphs. The most important thing any team can have is a person who can interpret what these graphs mean and who can then relate it back to the team and the drivers in an understandable language, telling them what changes need to be made to the car and how the driver can improve in driving the car. Anyone can look at the information— the information doesn't change—but not everyone can interpret the information to see that you're shifting gears too soon or hitting the brakes too late. Poor interpretation in racing can cost you a championship. Poor medical interpretation can cost you your life.

As we know, human error is rampant everywhere. We've spoken at length about the flaws in our governance systems, and there's no need to go on further, except to say that Jevitty is dedicated to innovating around them. Fortunately, bureaucracy and bad policy are a regional thing. Longevity, meanwhile, is global, and we will go wherever we need to go to get the job done.

If there's a new technology being hamstrung in Canada, we'll invest in the United States. If it's being hamstrung in the States, we'll invest in Switzerland, and so on. (As long as the work being undertaken is ethical, of course.) That's why we have the Jevitty Venture Fund investing in companies all over the world. We're investing in private companies and publicly traded companies in different geographic areas and in dynamic, widespread areas of interest, all toward companies and people doing great things for our future potential, health, and longevity.

We can't worry or think too much about the people or the systems who are blind to the necessary rate of progress. Innovation will always win out and spread across the globe once it does. Like when heart transplants became a viable technology in South Africa with Dr. Christiaan Barnard back in the 1970s. It happened in South Africa because they had the policies in place that allowed it to happen. Then, once the procedure was proven to work, policies changed around the world. Innovation will go where it needs to go in order to thrive. Today you might have somebody in South Africa doing things that aren't yet legal in the United States or Canada, but once they've accomplished and are successful at it, everyone else goes, "Huh. Maybe we'll try that out too." The more governments get on board with the concept of longevity, the easier it will be.

Smooth navigation is key, as is not getting worked up about the guys in the rear-view mirror. Why look back when you can focus forward? That's why we're finding all sorts of different ways to support innovation and health. Besides our Jevitty Venture Fund, we just launched the first Jevitty Brain Sponsorship. Our first order of business is sponsoring a local chess tournament, and we will be present to cheer on participants from all generations. This is something we haven't had a chance to address—how important it is to exercise your brain. We know that chess promotes brain-power and the prolongation of mental acuity, and research has shown that chess may help combat the onset of Alzheimer's and other neurodegenerative diseases. As such, this is an amazing integrative opportunity for us. We get to support a community event centred around improving our brains, and we get the Jevitty name out there.

We also recently sponsored a fundraiser for the Heart and Stroke Foundation and are constantly on the lookout for new ways to integrate, innovate, and improve the lives of the people around us. Staying open to opportunities keeps us fresh and engaged. You never know where the next paradigm-shifting idea is going to come from, and building community is always beneficial. It could be access to brain-powering events like chess tournaments that inspires a young entrepreneur to launch their first business, or it could be something as simple as two strangers meeting during a group run that brings together different perspectives to create something new. It's all about creating spaces for people to thrive, deepen connection, and find new ways to build and grow together.

Just like there are biotech companies repurposing orphan drugs for new uses, we're also keeping our eyes open for ways to innovate through repurposing what we already have. We don't always have to build something brand new to be innovative. There are so many creative ways to push the boundaries forward, and we want to be involved in all of them. We don't know where the next big breakthrough will come from. We just know that it's coming fast.

We haven't even scratched the surface of all the incredible innovations happening in health care and medicine today. Phenomenal breakthroughs, especially in the last twenty years, have completely changed the landscape of biological innovation. For example, in 2000, it took ten years and cost $3 billion to complete the first sequencing of a human genome (Cullis). By 2015, the cost was down to $1000 and the timeline took a day or two. In 2022, the whole human genome was sequenced for $100 in just over five hours (Pennisi). How long before it costs $10 … $0.10? How long before it takes only minutes … seconds?

Not only can we sequence our genome, but we've also figured out how to edit it too. This is thanks to the advent of CRISPR technology—technology that is changing everything. CRISPR (short for "clustered regularly interspaced short palindromic repeats") is a technology that scientists use to selectively modify the DNA of living organisms. The possibilities of CRISPR are astounding. As of 2019, researchers believed that this DNA editing technology would be able correct up to 89% of known genetic variants associated with human diseases (Gallagher). It is delivering promising results for diseases like sickle cell, and blood and lymph cancers including leukemia—and the door is wide open to tackle heart disease, muscular dystrophy, Alzheimer's, Parkinson's, Huntington's, and the list goes on and on ... This is clearly just the beginning. Between gene editing technology and stem cell technology, we'll be laughing all the way to two hundred.

Speaking of stem cell technology, researchers have developed a technique called iPSC—induced pluripotent stem cell—reprogramming, which is the process by which almost any somatic cell can be converted into an embryonic cell–like state. This is exactly the kind of groundbreaking technology that is going to allow us to reverse the process of aging, and it's already happening.

Preliminary research published in *eLife* now shows that it is possible to engineer human skin cells to reverse thirty years of aging, resetting skin cells to a youthful state. The method, called "maturation phase transient reprogramming," stops the process before the stem cell stage is reached, allowing the cell to retain its original identity and function.

A cure for type 1 diabetes is on the horizon, with one patient already potentially cured (Kolata). The experimental procedure uses injections of cells grown from the patient's own stem cells to get the pancreas to begin producing its own insulin again. Patients treated in this manner still have to take drugs to suppress their immune system as the body tries to attack the new cells, but scientists are exploring ways around this, including experiments with making the injected cells opaque—invisible to the immune system (ABCNews).

Meanwhile, platelet-rich plasma injections are gaining popularity. This treatment uses a patient's own blood cells to accelerate healing in damaged areas—with a particular focus on chronic tendon injuries in the knees and elbows.

A company called LyGenesis that focuses on tissue and organ regeneration is using patients' lymph nodes as bioreactors to enable organ regeneration—including growing new livers within their own bodies. Still in clinical trials, this technology could be revolutionary for the thousands of people awaiting organ transplants and the future of organ regeneration.

Stanford University has reported that they have developed an inoculation that significantly lowers the rates at which mice suffered from breast, lung, and skin cancers, demonstrating that we can use the immune system to kill cancer cells. It stands to reason that scientists will be able to figure out how to develop this technology to kill senescent cells too.

AI technology is detecting disease at earlier stages than human doctors have ever been able to. An artificial intelligence system developed at MIT is flagging signs of disease that are often invisible to the naked eye and using algorithms to predict—and thereby mitigate—patients' risks of developing cancer (Svoboda).

These are just a handful of examples. The rate of progress is staggering. And for every medical breakthrough, there are just as many more experimental techniques underway, pushing the edges of what's possible.

I've visited longevity labs and tested out some of their machines. There are so many incredible techniques and experiments and procedures available these days. I've tried ozone therapy, electrotherapy, negative chamber therapy. I did a "cold hit" machine that was almost like a cross-country trainer machine but you're seated and your feet are on cold plates. They put cold cups on your arms and legs and neck, pressurize you, and stimulate lactic acid production. Twelve minutes in that machine is like spending four hours hiking straight up a steep incline. I did negative chamber therapy, where you get in this little pod, kind of like a Solo, and it simulates ten thousand feet of altitude, as if your body was getting shot up in the air. Then it goes down to two thousand, then back up to ten thousand, and back down to two thousand, again and again for forty-five minutes. Let me tell you, the experience was not fun. But oh boy, do you sleep like a puppy afterward. The theory is that the changes in altitude compress and decompress your cells—every cell in your body right down to the stem cells— as a kind of regenerative therapy.

These places are like a little Disneyland for your body, and no doubt these labs and experimental techniques will continue to spring forth. Yes, at a cost. For now. While the most important longevity factors are within everyone's reach (sleep, food, exercise), the bells and whistles will only be available to the rich at first. Same as air travel, cars, computers, or any type of early innovation. That may be the case for the first anti-aging vaccines as well. Who knows? We'll see. It's also possible for the medicine to be democratized and distributed to the masses. It depends on who's behind the breakthrough. Jeff Bezos has recently launched a company to conquer aging. It's probably only a matter of time before Elon Musk gets with the program—and hopefully our governments too. Whoever champions this progress, they have my support.

While each passing day gives me more confidence that I will succeed in my goal—making it to two hundred years old with very little fanfare—I did speak with my friend Andrew Weaver, the climate scientist and former leader of the BC Green Party, before wrapping up this book. I wanted to ask his opinion on the state of the climate and what's in store for us. Sadly, he was not very optimistic. Though he still has hope, Andrew suggested that the future might not be pretty, offering a vision along the lines of "imploding revolutions." Yikes.

On the upside, what he reminded me of after all the doom and gloom is what we must focus on: the fact that the solutions do exist. All of them. We have all the tools and knowledge we need to tackle the climate and ecological crisis. It's all been charted and mapped out. We are not wanting for answers on how to fix things. All we need is the collaboration and willpower to see the changes through, which, in part, means overcoming the bureaucratic structure of government. As well as greed. And delusion. And human error—or human "nature" if that's what you want to call it.

While lack of government willpower and constant bickering between partisan parties—who seem to be more determined to protect their ideological identities than to work together on actual solutions—can make one feel defeated, Andrew reminded me of the most hopeful aspect of climate change: recognizing it as the single greatest opportunity the world has ever seen to innovate, to come together under a common goal, to be bold and creative and visionary, and to follow through on our Big Hairy Audacious Goals.

There is no excuse for any of us to not stand up and pursue our missions. Not anymore.

While nobody is bragging about gas cars anymore and we've passed a tipping point with electric cars, we still have to lean into being aggressively green. We know it's not enough to just shop at a local farmers' market (though it's a great thing to do), but that we must also take a hard look at globalization and trade and begin to account for the externalities—all the costs that have been hidden by corporations and global trade that we are now paying for as a collective. We must take seriously the possibility of the food chain breaking and invest in localized food security. We've got to buy up the Walmarts and the Exxons and convert them into plant-based corporations. We have to get serious about tackling this problem creatively, using the economic systemic to our—and everyone else's—benefit. Maybe that's capitalism becoming conscious and empathetic, or maybe there's a better economic model that retains the freedom of innovation that capitalism allows but finds a better way to get people who are sleeping out on the street into homes with food and health care and supervision or wraparound services if they need them. We can look to countries around the world leading in these areas and learn to emulate them. We have to approach the problem from all angles and not shy away from using the current systems to our advantage. We must understand that people, planet, and profit all have to work together for real sustainability.

There are also new systems like green banks that we could implement right away to support innovation on a mass scale. According to my friend and running buddy, Cam Brewer, the Bank of Canada is looking into this. The plan is to have green banks across Canada, places where anyone with a good, clean idea can get funding to innovate. Whether it's equity or patient capital, low interest loans, forgivable loans, or something backstopped by the government, there would be financing readily available to help entrepreneurs with their missions.

A green economy is the future, which means separating big industrial capitalism and the big corporate structures from the entrepreneurial spirit. We want to foster and uplift the innovation, not dampen it in any way. As Cam explains, in the context of co-ops and community ownership and green banks and Indigenous-owned businesses and initiatives, if you do these things in a serious way, outcomes can change quickly—and do we ever need that rapid, effective change. Because the way things are currently set up just doesn't make sense.

We are operating so inefficiently on the planet. Up to half of the food produced goes to waste (Institute of Mechanical Engineers). Americans use 250 times more water than they need. We treat sickness first instead of health. Industry after industry pumps out cheap products designed to fall apart. We have to disincentivize all of this behaviour.

The solutions don't need to be dramatic or difficult. In fact, it's better if they're not. The best solutions are simple. Elegant. Whenever possible, we must orient toward obsolescence. Reduce. Reuse. Create products that last. Longevity is the goal, right?

True longevity means living in symbiosis with the planet and with each other. That is the only way we all make it to our two-hundredth birthday.

The cure for aging is just around the corner, and with it comes exponential change in all directions. As David Sinclair says, "This is not just the start of a revolution; it is the start of an evolution". We truly can't even fathom what will come next. How fortunate are we to be alive here and now, watching the most dramatic shift in human evolution unfold? And while it doesn't come without challenges—frustration, pushback, and naysayers—what these tensions offer is the most dynamic opportunity for growth and visionary creation and innovation that humans have ever had the honour to witness and participate in.

There is so much to build and so much to change. It's hard to imagine what's beyond all the work we have ahead. What happens after we close the last gas station and solve aging? Your guess is as good as mine. The only thing I know for sure is that there'll always be more curiosity, more adventures, and more missions. Oh, and parties on Mars. Sounds like fun, doesn't it? I hope to see you there.

EPILOGUE

I would like to thank you, the reader, for your interest in the topic of inspirational entrepreneurship and for hopefully finding some spark of courage that will benefit yourself, your friends, your family, and perhaps even the world. I would also like to thank all the people who I've met, done business with, worked with, and interacted with over the years. All of you have in some way taught me something about the world we live in and how the people on it think. This includes my own family, with whom I shared our greenhouse business life for my first twenty-two years. Finally, I would like to thank my co-writer Kelly Tatham who shares many of my life principles and goals. She helped me make this book an interesting and useful device that I think will connect with anyone who believes they have something great inside themselves that needs to come out and become real. Thanks for being here and we'll see you next time!

WORKS CITED

BC Health Care Matters, https://bchealthcarematters.com/

Barzilai, Nir, and Toni Robino. "Unraveling the Longevity Mystery Deep Inside Our Cells ."

Age Later: Health Span, Life Span, and the New Science of Longevity, Thorndike Press, a Part of Gale, a Cengage Compnay, Waterville, ME, 2021

Byrne, Brendan. Interview. 20 May 2022.

Cullis, Pieter. *The Personalized Medicine Revolution: How Diagnosing and Treating Disease*

Are about to Change Forever. Greystone Books Ltd., 2015.

Döpfner, Mathias. "Elon Musk Discusses the War in Ukraine and the Importance of Nuclear

Power - and Why Benjamin Franklin Would Be 'the Most Fun at Dinner'." *Business Insider*, Business Insider, 26 Mar. 2022, https://www.businessinsider.com/elon-musk-interview-axel-springer-tesla-war-in-ukraine-2022-3.

Einstein, Albert, and Michael Amrine. "The Real Problem Is in the Hearts of Men." *The New*

York Times, The New York Times, 23 July 1946, https://timesmachine.nytimes.com/timesmachine/1946/06/23/issue.html.

Gallagher, James. "Prime Editing: DNA Tool Could Correct 89% of Genetic Defects." *BBC*

News, BBC, 21 Oct. 2019, https://www.bbc.com/news/
health-50125843.

Gill, Diljeet, and Aled Parry. "Multi-Omic Rejuvenation of
Human Cells by Maturation Phase

Transient Reprogramming." *ELife*, 8 Apr. 2022

"GLOBAL FOOD: WASTE NOT, WANT NOT," Institute of
Mechanical Engineers, January

10, 2013 https://www.imeche.org/docs/default-source/
news/Global_Food_Waste_Not_Want_Not.
pdf?sfvrsn=7b0bfb7d_0. Accessed 20 Feb 2023.

Kolata, Gina. "A Cure for Type 1 Diabetes? for One Man, It Seems
to Have Worked." *The New*

York Times, The New York Times, 27 Nov. 2021, https://www.
nytimes.com/2021/11/27/health/diabetes-cure-stem-cells.
html.

"Man Temporarily Cured of Type 1 Diabetes." YouTube, ABC
News, 3 Dec. 2021,

https://www.youtube.com/watch?v=dGRzVyj3vPw.

"Pesticide Concerns in Cotton." Pesticide Action Network UK, 20
June 2022,

https://www.pan-uk.org/cotton/

Pennisi, Elizabeth "A $100 Genome? New DNA Sequencers
Could Be a 'Game Changer' for

Biology, Medicine." *Science*, 15 June 2022,

https://www.science.org/content/article/100-genome-new-dna-
sequencers-could-be-game-changer-biology-medicine.

Rutherford, Gillian. "Excess Sugar Costs Canada $5 Billion Each Year: Study." *University of*

Alberta, 16 Mar. 2022, https://www.ualberta.ca/folio/2022/03/ excess-sugar-consumption-costs-canadas-health-care-system-5-billion-each-year.html.

Sinclair, David, director. *David Sinclair: Is Aging Reversible? A Scientific Look with David*

Sinclair | TED Talk, 15 Mar. 2022, https://www.ted.com/talks/ david_sinclair_is_aging_reversible_a_scientific_look_with_ david_sinclair. Accessed 28 Feb. 2023.

Sinclair, David, and Matthew D. LaPlante. "The Shape of Things to Come ." *Lifespan: Why We*

Age and Why We Don't Have To, Harper Thorsons, London, 2021.

Svoboda, Elizabeth. "A Closer Look." *Discover Science*, July 2022, pp. 32–35.

Zaraska, Marta. "Perspective | Boosting Our Sense of Meaning in Life Is an Often Overlooked

Longevity Ingredient." *The Washington Post*, WP Company, 3 Jan. 2021, https://www.washingtonpost.com/health/ boosting-our-sense-of-meaning-in-life-is-an-often-over-looked-longevity-ingredient/2020/12/31/84871d32-29d4-1 1eb-8fa2-06e7cbb145c0_story.html.

Printed in the USA
CPSIA information can be obtained
at www.ICGtesting.com
LVHW041604241223
766817LV00004BA/6/J